Free Computers

To Lisa:
Waves and roses.

Free Computers

A
Simple Guide
to Building a Working
Computer from Scavenged Parts

James MacLaren

PALADIN PRESS • BOULDER, COLORADO

Free Computers: A Simple Guide to Building a Working Computer from Scavenged Parts
by James MacLaren

Copyright © 2004 by James MacLaren

ISBN 1-58160-455-6
Printed in the United States of America

Published by Paladin Press, a division of
Paladin Enterprises, Inc.
Gunbarrel Tech Center
7077 Winchester Circle
Boulder, Colorado 80301 USA
+1.303.443.7250

Direct inquiries and/or orders to the above address.

Visit our Web site at www.paladin-press.com

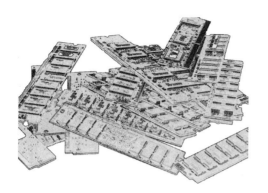

Table of Contents

Warning

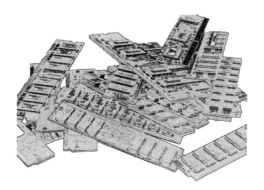

Some of the techniques discussed in this book, particularly those involving monitors and components that hold an electrical charge, can be extremely dangerous. It is not the intent of the author or publisher to encourage readers to attempt any of them without proper professional supervision and training. Attempting to do so can result in severe injury or death.

The author, publisher, and distributors of this book disclaim any liability from any damage or injuries of any type that a reader or user of information contained within this book may incur from the use of said information. *This book is for academic study only.*

Acknowledgments

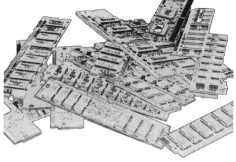

Thanks to all:

CBSC	WordPerfect
Richard Walls	Kai MacLaren
Eugene Hajdaj	The Ref
Robert Strickland	Bill Gates
Symtek Computers	Steve Jobs
Beach Computers	Linus Torvalds
Jim Holsonback	Luther Broome
Bev Freed	MCF
Wayne Sarosi	Francis MacLaren
Mark Spivey	Blanche Julia Pickels
Barbara Louise Bailey	The "Oh Wow"
Debbie Knight	Dennis Eichhorn
Sprocket	Michael Hoy
Julio Cicconi	Lilly Golden
Jerry Russell	Jon Ford
Ray Edester	Dick Hinshaw
George Drazich	Dom Salemi
FidoNet	Reverend Randall Tin-ear
PC Tools	Kim Cooper
WordStar	Ian Koss

Univac   Harry Solana
IBM   Howard J. Petty
Milspec Contracting   The Baby Bird
Corporation   Carl Colvenbach
Launch Complex 39B   Mavis Beacon
Launch Complex 41   John Muir
Ivey Construction   Air Force Missile Test Center
Sheffield Steel   Erik Anderson
Jan Hoover   Wes Dobry
Ben Dusenberry   Michael Faraday
David Spain   Miss Piggy
JoAnn Grentner   Harry Gant
Slashdot   Dennis DiCicco

Apologies to those worthies that I missed. I'm getting old. My brain isn't as crisp as it used to be. Or maybe it's crisper. Dunno.

How to Use This Book

Even though I advise you to read this thing through from start to finish before picking up a screwdriver, that's not absolutely required. If you're curious about what a modem (or whatever) is, then read the part on modems (or whatever). If you're lucky, that might be all you need to read. But don't count on it, OK? Just go ahead and read it all the way through one time to make *me* happy and then jump in on whatever part seems most relevant when the hardware is strewn across the kitchen countertop. You'll be glad you did it that way.

No two computers are going to be alike. No two people working on the same computer are going to be alike. Expect things to be a little different when it's *your* turn. Even though things will be a little different, a liberal application of your street smarts will see you through whatever problem you've stumbled upon. Look for similarities, not exact matches. *Be willing to improvise, adapt, and overcome.* Be willing to play with things, even to the point of breaking them. Learn to laugh it off. Learn to laugh at yourself. Learn to laugh.

The importance of your social skills cannot be overemphasized. Brush up on them if you need to. Otherwise, no free computer for you, my friend.

Electricity can be dangerous. You already know that. Be careful.

But more than anything else, *HAVE FUN WITH THIS!*

Chapter 1 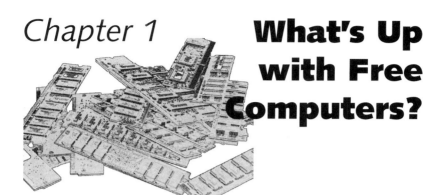 **What's Up with Free Computers?**

Free computers? Yeah right, sure thing. Hell, there's hardly even any free *calculators* out there!

Or at least this is what most folks think, anyway. But it's not true. Despite the fact that people routinely pay thousands of dollars for a desktop computer, the world abounds with free computers. It's awash in the damned things, in fact. The guys who run the landfills are having problems with disposing of all the computer carcasses they get each and every day. Fact is, most of these "carcasses" are no such thing. They are fully functioning, or partially functioning, really-o, truly-o, by golly computers!

Whaddaya say we do our bit to keep the landfill from becoming overrun with the things by grabbing them off, every chance we get?

But don't go thinking that we're just Dumpster diving here, OK? The trash angle is a valid one, but it's only a tiny part of the overall picture of free computers. There's a whole world of free computers out there, lurking in hidden nooks and crannies that we can avail ourselves of. Think of free computers as big game that we must hunt down. Our prey is cunning, and if we are to return home with a trophy, we must use every trick in the book to help us bag the beast. This little book will show you how to do it. Successfully. Repeatedly.

Let's go.

WHY YOU MIGHT WANT YOUR COMPUTER FOR FREE, INCLUDING THE UNOBVIOUS REASONS

Sounds like a dumb question on the face of it, but then so do a lot of other questions. Why indeed?

Just to get it out of the way, the obvious reason is that it's always better to get something for nothing, right? No-brainer there. But there's more.

An unobvious reason is that free things are much easier to tinker around with. No worries about breaking something that cost you two months' pay. I'll get into this in far greater detail later on. For now, it's enough to know that your free computer will liberate you to learn about it in ways that a rig costing hundreds or thousands of dollars simply will not permit.

Yet another unobvious reason is one of traceability. Or, to be more precise, the lack thereof. Yes indeed, boys and girls, there's people out there doing things with computers that they'd rather not have the whole world (or even their credit card company) knowing about. One way to ensure that you're working in a better grade of isolation is to glom onto your computer for free—no paper, no proof of purchase, no nuthin'. This also extends to the software your free computer comes loaded with. Just don't go calling up customer support when you have a question about that software, OK? The guy on the other end of the phone might not take too kindly to your query and start tapping keys and filling in blanks on some form in a way that you might not like.

Talk of software leads directly to talk of data. You *would not believe* some of the stuff I've found on the hard drives of cast-off computers: credit card numbers, bank account numbers, Social Security numbers, medical records, intimate personal stuff, legal stuff. Stuff that a competing business would give *serious money* to have. Hell, there's no end to it! People are IDIOTS! They go to extraordinary lengths to safeguard their property, and then turn around and do something spectacularly stupid like leaving the combination to the padlock on their storage unit in plaintext, in a clearly labeled file, in a computer that they wind up tossing. Data you can extract from an old hard drive comes in many layers of increasing difficulty to recover, but the bottom line is that all of it is recoverable by one means or another if the person doing the recovery work has enough resources. And yes, the NSA and several other equally cheerful outfits have more than the requisite amount of resources.

The above notwithstanding, mind your karma, OK? The Dark Side exerts a powerful appeal to certain types of people, but it always brings them down hard before all's said and done. Many people never make the connection between their own rotten luck and the fact that they're always attempting to cut corners and get over on their fellow humans. Try to stay out of *that* group every chance you get.

Free computers, in and of themselves, come with no karma or even *positive* karma (we'll get into that in much greater detail later on too). But taking things like credit card numbers and then using them to *steal* from their owners will inevitably bring evil fortune to those who do it. Don't do it.

YOU *CAN* GET SOMETHING FOR NOTHING, BUT DON'T GO EXPECTING A CADILLAC, OK?

OK, time for a little cold water in the face. A reality check, as it were. Yes, you CAN get a free computer. A whole room full of them in fact. All shapes and sizes. But no, you're *not* going to get some kind of Cray behemoth that's capable of teraflopping its way to predicting the weather a month from now. What you *can* get is a rig that will perform many useful tasks so long as you don't ask too much of it. Try not to ask too much of *anything* as you travel down the Road of Life, OK? It's better that way.

People do not spend a couple of grand on a rig and then just decide to give it away to the next homeless guy they meet walking down the boulevard. You would think that common sense would cover this bit of obvious information, but my experience with folks leads me to believe otherwise. And, incredibly, some folks, upon discovering that they can't get the latest model for nada, get all pissy about that fact. Like a greedy little kid pitching a fit in the store because mama got him a plastic bucket and shovel to go dig holes in the beach sand with instead of a brand-new surfboard.

Whenever I cross paths with this sort of individual, my inclination to give them a free computer drops to zero. (Giving the things away is the heart and soul of what we're going to be doing here, as you shall soon see.) Good people get a good deal. Selfish people get to continue whining because they didn't get a good deal. The person doing the giving is judge, jury, and executioner. No right to appeal. And please don't try to fake your way through this one, OK? Yes, you'll get over on some folks sometimes. But no, you're not doing yourself any favors in the long run.

Take what little life chooses to give to you with a glad heart and a cheerful attitude. The Fountain of Free Things is like a pump that needs priming. You've got to put a little something into the deal to get something back out. The higher the quality of what you put in, the higher the quality of what comes back out.

I still can't believe that I've got to tell people this kind of thing. It's just too obvious. But for some reason, nobody wants to be bothered with the nitty-gritty details of conducting themselves honorably with their fellow man.

All of the above may sound like sheerest padding, having nothing to do with acquiring free computers and everything to do with a third-rate author clumsily attempting to fill out an entire book's worth of space with words, any words, but that's not the case at all. I'm attempting to adjust your attitude here. A well-tuned attitude is the key to everything that follows—I cannot overemphasize this crucial point. We are dealing with people, not computers. With a few minor exceptions, we're going to have to interact with a living, breathing, caring person in order to score our free rig. If that living, breathing person does not care, then you can forget about it; you must cause people to care about you to pull this off. Any kind of blemish on your attitude or behavior is going to wreck your chances. People will pick up on that kind of thing instantly, and they will not give you a second chance. They know other folks who are worthier. Strive to become as worthy as you can. This will bring you good things for the rest of your life if you can figure it out. The free computers will become the merest of gravy.

WE'RE TALKING PCs HERE, NOT MACS, AND WHILE WE'RE AT IT, SKIP THE SCSI AND THE LAPTOP TOO

I suppose, before I go any further, that I ought to advise you about what sorts of computers you can *reasonably* expect to be getting for free. In addition to the Cray, you're unlikely to see anything by Apple. Exactly why this is, I'm not entirely sure. Over the years I've been given literally hundreds of machines and thousands of pieces and parts. Of this entire trove, about three machines and a similar number of parts have been by Apple. All of those machines were either so ancient and primitive that my pocket calculator could outperform them or just completely ruined and worthless. (Try not to lay your wet, salty, sandy wetsuit on top of the computer after a day of surfing, OK?)

Apple people are weird and that's about all you can say about it. They *love* their machines dearly and apparently cannot bear to part with the damned things no matter how obsolete or useless they become. Apple people are also fanatics, and when dealing with fanatics, logic and reason take a backseat, if they're even on the bus at all. (Watch—I'll get mail, soaked with foam from around the guy's mouth, that rages at me about how Apple people are *not* fanatics.)

This is a shame really, since Apples are excellent computers, vastly superior to your standard PC in many, many ways. But as long as they remain in the clutches of their slightly deranged owners, it's not doing you or me a whit of good. Too bad, eh?

And while we're discussing Apples here, we may as well talk about working on them. In a word, they're pesty. Your typical PC is almost always a promiscuously tolerant machine, willing to accept most anything you might take a notion to shove into its slots and receptacles. Not so, Apples. They're extremely fussy about what they will accept. (Read: nothing whatsoever, including other Apple parts, unless those parts are *just so.*) This fussiness makes for a much more difficult time of it when you're scavenging around in a pile of wires, chips, cards, funny-looking little doodads, and all the rest of it when attempting to assemble, something, ANYTHING, that will just work fer chrissakes.

Apples are further hobbled by a software system that steadfastly refuses to allow you to "look under the hood" without recourse to the full panoply of spells, incantations, magic runes, and perhaps a sacrificial chicken, still twitching on the altar, headless. Apples are designed from the ground up to be extraordinarily easy on the user, requiring zero by way of tweakery to keep them humming right along. The payback for this ease of use is that if you ever want to diddle around with the innermost settings of the thing, you can pretty much forget it. And without the ability to diddle down deep, your chances of successfully kludging some found part or other onto your semicomplete machine plummet.

Something else to beware of is SCSI. No, I'm not going to tell you what it means. It's just another in the endless series of obfuscatory acronyms that computer geeks *love* to label things with. SCSI is pronounced by its devotees as "skuzzy." Perhaps they're attempting to tell us something? Dunno. What I do know is that SCSI is nonstandard in the

world of free computers. And anything nonstandard is likely to spend a whale of a lot of time on the shelf waiting for
something to come along that matches it. THIS you do not
want. Go ahead and accept all SCSI rigs and parts with
good grace and don't throw them away. You might get
lucky and manage to assemble a fully functioning computer using SCSI compatible parts (hard drives, for the most
part). And if you do, the thing will just sing and dance for
you. SCSI works really well. But you can grow old and gray
waiting for that final piece to come along and complete
your machine.

And finally, beware of free laptops. Especially ones that
almost, but don't quite, work. Older laptops in particular are
a real pain in the hemorrhoids to work with. On a laptop
everything is nonstandard. Go ahead and keep the laptop,
but don't put it on top of your stack of parts and pieces.
(I've got three of the bastards right this minute, languishing
away waiting for the magic component to arrive and make
things all better.) Additionally, laptops are just a major bother to even open up and work on. All sorts of dippy hidden
latches and sneakily camouflaged screws and fasteners. And
even after you succeed in getting the thing open without
breaking it, you're faced with its innards, which are even
worse. Phoo.

What all of the above boils down to is this: Concentrate
on PCs. There's more of 'em. They get replaced more often,
thus freeing up their older brethren to fall into your clutches. They also crap out more often (almost always single-
point failures easily fixable by replacing a single doodad). If
your first free computer is some kind of weird-ass thing
with nonstandard everything, go ahead and work it over
and figure it out. Just don't go letting it persuade you that
all other machines will be the same or even remotely
resemble it.

If you don't know the difference between a PC and anything else, just check for an Apple label. If it doesn't have
one, then it's a PC. Easy, huh?

Exceptions to What I Just Said

OK, now that I've got you thinking that it's strictly a PC deal, I'm going to attempt to persuade you otherwise. Nice of me, eh?

In the ever-changing world of personal computers, stuff becomes obsolete and suddenly starts arriving on your doorstep for free with bewildering speed. Laptops are an excellent case in point. Owing to their restrictive nature, laptops generally come fresh from the factory just about as cram-packed with hardware and software as they can tolerate. When a new operating system (or even better, a new *game*) comes along that simply will not fit on what mere months ago was a perfectly good machine, certain people are going to ditch that machine in favor of something that will properly ingest this latest, greatest thing. Should the latest, greatest thing be some new physical hardware gizmo, things get even better. Not only is it likely that the poor soon-to-be-orphaned machine is not blessed with the *space* to put that hardware in, it's also quite likely that it's not blessed with the ability to deal with that hardware *on any terms* from an operational point of view.

And so, even though it's still fully functional, its owner forsakes it. This is good news for you and me. Folks who buy laptops have money—the damned things are *not* inexpensive. And when Mister Owner attempts to sell his used laptop, he runs right into the brick wall of other laptop users, none of whom would be caught dead without the latest, thinnest, lightest, most high-poweredest whindangdoo on the market. These folks are not going to shell out a grand, or even a couple of hundred, to pick up this used machine. They have other things in their sights and the jack in their pocket to bring 'em home. And so, our laptop languishes in the closet, unused, until one fine day Mister Owner has had to move the stupid thing one too many times to get to the tennis racquets underneath it and decides to just chuck it.

If you have recently inquired as to any "dead" machines lying around, then the odds are *excellent* that Mister Owner will just sort of roll over, play dead, and hand it over.

Cool, huh?

Another laptop buzzkill is the dead battery. When you check the prices on replacement batteries, be ready for some serious sticker shock. (If you have to keep it wired to a wall socket in order to use it, then the whole purpose of owning a laptop sort of disappears.) And, natch, none of 'em are cross-compatible with other laptops, even ones with the same brand name. With just one or two exceptions, all of my free laptops have arrived in this condition. In fact, the machine I wrote my previous title, *Learn to Surf*, on was just such a machine. For myself, not being some kind of high-powered Republican mover and shaker—who must be ever-enabled to do whatever them nitwits do with their array of electronic gizmos 24 hours a day, even when they're in the shower fer chrissakes—I'm just as happy as a clam to use a laptop that's plugged into a wall socket. Especially when it comes to Internet connections, which (for the most part) require me to be plugged into the wall anyhow.

I dunno what's up with them people, but the fact that they're out there at all causes manna from heaven to fall out of the sky and land at my feet. Nice, that.

The above remarks about new hardware coming along that a not-so-old machine is simply unable to deal with also applies to standard-issue PCs. Just not nearly as much.

Cast-off machines from businesses can arrive in almost any incarnation. I've dealt with more than a few servers from banks and places like that. Servers rock! They're possessed of some serious horsepower. They're also usually just as weird and nonstandard as they can be. If you get one, pray that it's still functional. Parts for servers do not grow on trees.

OK. Enough of this noise. When's the book start?

WHAT THIS BOOK CONTAINS AND HOW YOU WILL MAKE USE OF IT

OK, now we're getting somewhere. Whaddaya say we

talk about what's in this thing and what's in it for you?

And when you boil it down, it's not much, really—just your technical skills and your social skills. Two items, plus a few tidbits that don't fit squarely into either category but aren't worthy of being given their own category.

We've already seen a little bit about social skills, so you're already well aware of where we're gonna be going with that one. And I've deliberately thrown some technical lingo at you just to get you used to the fact that we're entering a strange little world with quirks and peculiarities all its very own. (And no, it doesn't matter in the least if you've completely failed to understand the lingo you've seen so far. It's just a bunch of gobbledygook for the most part. You'll do fine without it, but any that you manage to absorb through the pores of your skin as you read this thing will be an asset. Just don't get your piss in a boil if you're not grokking it instantly as each new word swims by on the page.)

Relax. This stuff's nowheres near as complicated as the legion of computer weenies would like you to believe it is. After all, them mopes are doing this *for a living*. It's putting coffee in their cups and beer in their coolers. They would prefer it if you didn't come along and mess up the system that allows them to put on the wizard's hat and pluck $50s from the wallets of idiots like so many salted peanuts from a bag.

Who can blame 'em?

Your Technical Skills

To elaborate a little bit more on your technical skills, allow me to reiterate the fact that you really don't need any.

How I'm Going to Approach the Subject of Technical Matters

We need to get sorted out on something before I really plunge in to all this crap, and that's the detailed business of how I'm going to approach technical matters.

Technical matters. Eewww.

Nobody likes it (at least not anybody normal).

Stop for a minute here and consider any or all of those little booklets (and more than just a few full-tilt tomes) that show up in the box your new electronic device was packed inside of. Can anybody read any of this stuff? Judging from the fact that most people can't even set the clock on their VCR, my guess is no. The only people who can read the damned instruction book are the folks who built the electronic device and maybe a couple of buttholes from the legal department. What's up with that? So here we go with yet another book about how to operate some damned electric gizmo or other—the book you hold in your hands right this second.

A rant on book-writing engineers and their friends, if you will:

As a general rule, the people who write this kind of stuff are *proud* of the fact that they couldn't spell "cat" if you spotted 'em the c and the t. Engineers. Some of the dumbest people I've ever crossed paths with on this whole planet were engineers. For whatever reason, they managed to pass calculus class and get their little degree in whatever arcane field of engineering and all of a sudden they know *everything*! All of it! Or at least that's what they believe in their own tiny brains.

You and I know better. Far better.

Engineers don't communicate worth a damn and don't seem to care. If they cared, I'm guessing they'd at least make a half-honest attempt to improve their communication skills. But none of 'em ever do.

And so, when it comes to the instructions and directives for building or fixing your computer, you run head-on into the sad fact that the bastard who created the document doesn't know how to operate his own native language, even when it's English. And on top of that, he never once in his life had to get his pudgy little fingers soiled with the grime that attaches itself to actual physical objects as they exist in the real world, thereby making him delusional as to the actual relationships that exist between those physical objects in the real world.

Screw him.

You and I, dear reader, are going to go about this business of putting things together a different way.

I don't have a legal department to send this thing to for all of that anointment, blessing, and general ring-kissing that legal departments seem so fond of. Which means I can just hammer right along without worrying about getting crosswise with the people who wrote the warranty or any of the bean counters they report to. Not only do we not have a warranty, we don't want one. That would only complicate matters. Screw that. Screw the engineers, screw the lawyers, and screw the bean counters.

There, doesn't that feel better?

A primary thought to keep in mind at all times when working on your free computer is that the damned thing was for free. Free, got it? If you break something, you haven't lost a nickel, have you? No, you have not.

This is heady stuff.

Real liberating.

Now that we're free as birds to just do any damned thing we want to, that's exactly what we're gonna do.

You are hereby permitted and *encouraged* to go ahead and jam part "A" into slot "B" just to see if it fits. And if it does fit, then plug it in and fire it up! See what it does. See if smoke and flames come out of it. What the hell, why not?

It's free!

You can learn an incredible amount with this freewheeling technique of computer assembly. If it blows itself to hell, you *will* remember what happened and never have to worry about what to do when a similar situation comes up. You'll *know*.

If it spins right up and starts painting pretty colors on the screen, cooing sweetly to you as it does, you will remember what happened and never have to worry about what to do when a similar situation comes up. You'll know.

Pretty bitchin', huh?

And, as a special bonus, once you get into the nitty-gritty of all this, you'll discover that the list of different types of slots and parts that go into them is amazingly short.

It's *standardized*.

Too cool!

A final bonus derives from the fact that almost all of the stuff you'll be working on is obsolete or damned close to it. (Don't let that scare you off. It still works and works well.) Since it's already been out there for years, everybody already knows all about it. There's a gondola carload of helpful folks out there who know every possible nuance regarding the nature of whatever conundrum is sitting on your kitchen table. And they just *love* to help out beginners. I don't know what it is about people who fiddle with electronic doodads, but almost every one of them is dying to help you out by passing along their store of arcane information to you.

Playground with playground equipment.

Nice that way, eh?

So you just drag the stuff into the house, split it open, pull the innards out, and then start playing around with it. And I do mean playing. Like a little kid with a bag of new toys. Whee! This is fun!

Which is the whole idea. If all this fooling around results in a functioning computer, then we're talking complete and utter gravy here.

Figure out how to hold on to your cheerful attitude about playing around with computer parts, OK? That attitude will work miracles.

No lie.

Social Skills

Ah, yes, your social skills. A very important matter.

At first glance, it seems more than just a little weird to be talking about somebody's social skills in a book about computers, but it turns out that your success with acquiring, assembling, and upgrading your free computer is directly related to your social skills, or lack of them.

Let's face it, people are nice to people they like, and not so nice to people they don't like. Simple enough, eh?

It all boils down to: How much fun are you to be around? If you're no fun to be around, nobody's going to let you glom onto his or her old computer. You will be reduced to getting everything from Dumpsters and the side of the street on trash pickup day. Which is not to say that you'll never ever put a free computer together, but it will take longer. Much longer.

So why not make things easier on yourself and improve your social skills? Hell, it just might come in handy somewhere else too.

We'll start by reminding you that you're asking people for a favor when you ask for their old computer. In order to get that favor, you're going to have to pay into the game somehow.

So right this minute start brushing up on your doing-people-favors skills. And don't go thinking about how they're going to have come across with a little something before you come across with the favor. Forget that. The whole deal revolves around your doing people favors *for no reason at all*. No, you don't have to give them your house or anything. Little stuff will do, but it's got to be from the heart. Helping folks with tasks they're doing is always a hit, especially anything that requires heavy lifting or dragging. No-brainer stuff. Help people at work. Help people when you're over at their place visiting. Help total strangers that you'll never see again in your life. After you've helped a tourist dig his car out of the soft sand while you were down in Florida for spring break, somebody you don't even know back home in Ohio will offer you a nice 17-inch monitor for no reason at all. Trust me here, this WORKS! Practice it.

Another social skill is the ability to refrain from telling folks how messed up they are. And this goes double when they really are messed up. Instead of pointing out the fact that their teeth stink, tell them they're smart or something. Keep the bad news to yourself. The only time when it's OK to tell people they're messed up is when you're trying to persuade them to kindly get out of your life and to please stay there. In that case, it's not only OK, it's actually DESIR-ABLE to tell people their teeth stink. Or whatever. Just don't plan on asking them about that old computer they haven't used in the last couple of years, OK?

And while we're at it, let's all try to be less messed up ourselves. Go brush those teeth, dammit.

If you have a sense of humor, use it. But be double damn sure you actually have a sense of humor. Idiots who attempt to be funny without paying close attention to the reactions they're getting in their audience are some of the most unpleasant people you can be around.

Oh hell, I could go on with this kind of thing for another hour. But what's the use? This ain't no psychology textbook. Just try to fix things up so that people leave your presence in a better mood than they were in when they first encoun-

tered you. Pay attention to their body language. Keep your
eyes open. Be ready to adjust to suit the individual. This
ain't rocket science here.

When people regard you as a source of fun and interest-
ing stuff, they'll start coming across with all sorts of little
stuff in exchange for your oh-so-pleasant company.

And no, you can't fake this one. People will sniff that
out faster than you can say, "Hey, where you going?" You've
got to be for real.

If your ego or whatever will not permit you to make
these little personal adjustments, you may as well put this
book down and plan on buying the damned computer.

All of the above also applies directly to your ability to
persuade people to help you when you're just learning what
the hell's going on inside a computer. Folks that have no
intention of giving you the time of day are hardly going to
be inclined to inform you how to tell at a glance if your
floppy-drive cable is plugged in backward, right?

"Hello," "goodbye," "please," "thank you," and "I'm sorry"
should not be alien concepts to your mind. Get comfortable
with this stuff if you're not already comfortable with it. It
doesn't cost a damn thing to operate these concepts, and
the rewards for a fluency in them cannot be overstated.

Be nice, dammit!

Don't Be In a Hurry

Alright then, what else can we gird your loins for battle
with? How 'bout your sense of timing? In particular, your
sense of being in a hurry or not.

Were we bagging some kind of perishable product like
fresh lettuce, I'd be going out of my way to tell you to hurry
up! But that's not what we're doing. The stuff we're after
keeps well in most any environment so long as it's not directly out in the weather. And as far as that goes, even a certain
amount of weather, even heavy weather, is not necessarily a
bad thing. And so our sense of urgency must be lopped off
when it comes to dealing with whatever comes our way.

Breathe deep. Take your time. Allow things to find you
on their time, not yours. Not only will this permit you to
take full advantage of your finds, it just might seep into
other areas of your life.

What's the hurry?

Enjoy what few days you may have left upon this orb of
mud and ashes. People, when faced with their ultimate
doom, never think of how much stuff they've got. It's
always friends and family, and how they love them and
how they wish they'd spent more time with them. This sort
of thing is sending you a message. Tune your receiver so
that you can pick it up.

The computer can wait.

Don't let your quest for free computers turn you into a
butthole.

And besides, people don't go giving buttholes free computers.

Don't Ever Throw Anything Away

One of the reasons you can afford to not be in a hurry is
that everything you've ever glommed onto is still sitting
around waiting for that magic moment when it suddenly
becomes not just useful, but even vital.

This is because you *never threw anything away*.

Make a note about that over in the margin, OK?

Again, with feeling, NEVER THROW ANYTHING AWAY.

Got a nice sound to it, don't it?

Computer gear seems to go through several phases during its tenure on Earth. It starts out as highly prized stuff,
sometimes worth more than its weight in gold. Somewhere
along the line the luster starts to fade, and it then drops to
merely good utility-grade stuff. At some point after that it
starts to transmogrify into trash. But then, some time beyond
that, it qualifies as "hard-to-get" stuff, kind of like an antique
or perhaps a collectible, and regains some of its value.

I suppose if the feds are banging on the front door even
as you're on your way out the back door, then it's OK to

lose the computer stuff. Or perhaps if your U-Haul is unable to accept one more thing—unless it's no larger than a postage stamp—on the morning of your cross-country move, then that would be a time to let some of it go.

But I'll guarantee you that within three months of watching your pile of parts get smaller and smaller in the rearview mirror, you'll have an urgent need for something or other that missed the boat. So as long as the stuff isn't a major source of marital discord, or perhaps has become the new home to a growing family of furry vermin, or is blocking access to other, more valuable stuff, then by all means hold on to it.

And there's more to it than merely still having the doodad required to complete a working computer.

As I type these words (early 2003), the long-heralded demise of the 3 1/4-inch floppy-disk drive seems to be upon us. The old 5 1/2-inch drives (the ones that were actually floppy) are already long gone. Along with the drives themselves, the disks and cabling that use them are becoming extinct too. Needless to say, I've got a respectable stash of the 5 1/2-inch drives and more than enough 3 1/4-inch drives. Once in a great while somebody that knows me will stumble across a pile of those old disks in the attic trunk of a dearly departed loved one. These people have *no way* to read those disks without one of my drives. Nine times out of 10, what gets found on those disks (assuming they're still readable) is work-related crap like old Lotus 1-2-3 spreadsheets or some damned business correspondence between boring people like lawyers and accountants. But every once in a great while, old letters between friends, family, or lovers once again flicker across the phosphors, momentarily breathing life of a sort into a bygone world long since wiped from the face of the Earth. Needless to say, when something like that happens, the cool-o-meter pegs its needle and people become MOST appreciative. Shoot it to the printer and voila! You've got an instant family heirloom. This sort of stuff falls under the heading of Priceless.

Because of the exact scenario described above, one must also *never* discard old software. Oftentimes, without the program that created it, an old item dredged up from the musty past remains completely inscrutable, defying all attempts to decipher the mysteries within.

In their rush to embrace the future, most folks can't throw away the past fast enough. This is not a good thing and can cause a sort of blindness to events both great and trifling that once loomed large in the lives of the blinded. It's up to guys like you and me to give these unknowing fools their sight back every so often.

Even Obviously Broken Things

Hard drives that make a loud rattling sound when powered on and fail to do anything other than cause your computer to give you a plaintive error message would appear to be obvious Dumpster fodder, right?

Wrong.

Ditto other trashed items.

Stuff that you can't imagine a use for just might fit the bill for the imagination of somebody else. So hang on to it, OK?

Weird and Silly Uses for Broken Computer Parts

Keep in mind here that this is just some of the stuff that *I* can think of. There's way more than this.

Dead hard drives are just cooler than cool once you've opened 'em up. Neat little roboto swing arms and shiny, shiny, shiny platters that spin around and around. Kids *love* 'em. Mind the toddlers, OK? But middle-size kids are always fascinated by the innards of a hard drive. Think cheap toys—REALLY cheap toys. Let one of the tykes take it to show and tell. She'll be the hit act of the day.

As far as it goes, a whole computer is a load of fun for a kid with a screwdriver and some time on her hands. Let her just take everything she can apart. But be double damn sure to either *remove* the power supply or *discharge* the filter condensers. And don't leave a power cord handy either.

With these sim-
ple precau-
tions, a kid can
spend days
putzing around
with the
innards of a
computer. Not
only is it fun, it
teaches 'em
about how
technical doo-
dads actually
go together,
and how to

Your hard drive's innards. (Spinning platter's motion frozen by high-speed flash.)

manipulate those very same technical doodads. Anything
that removes some of the mystery of this world to a young
person is a good thing. Might just spark a lifelong interest in
math and science. There's worse things that could happen
to a kid, eh?

The cards that fit into the slots on a motherboard can be
fun all by themselves too. No spinning whirligigs, but
they're just neat looking. For that matter, the whole damned
motherboard is too. Like some kind of space city in minia-
ture or something. Just hand it over all nonchalant and let
your child's imagination do the rest. Again, toddlers can
manage to poke themselves with some of this stuff, so
please exercise due caution. And for that matter, I don't
think I'd like seeing this stuff in a small child's mouth,
either—no telling what some of it is made of. But for hands-
on fun, it's probably better than some of the Star Wars stuff
that's out there. And you can't beat the price.

Another angle is art. As in fully grown adult-type persons using some of this whack-looking stuff to create . . .
who knows? For myself, I've always wanted to cover a car
in cards and motherboards—just buy a 5-gallon bucket of
epoxy and go to town with it. Somebody out there probably

Tot's-eye view of a really cool imaginary city, dust and all.

already has, and I'm just too ignorant to know about it. Are we getting the idea here yet? Just 'cause it's a broken thing doesn't mean that it no longer has ANY use or significance. Hell, I'm always hearing ancient, clunky computers called "boat anchors." Why not try it out and see? Or maybe just a nice doorstop. Whatever.

THE BASIC PREMISE: GIVING COMPUTERS AWAY

And now for the secret key to the whole damned operation; the fuel that runs the motor; the crucial concept, without which your ship of free computers shall surely founder on the reefs of bad luck and misfortune: You're going to be getting free computers because *you give computers away to worthy individuals in need of a little charity.*

Stop right here and go have a beer and watch some trash TV or something. Maybe go check the oil in your car. Go distract yourself. Let this concept seep into the back of your brain while the front of your brain is occupied elsewhere. I'll wait right here for you.

Hum de dum, la dee da, doo doo doo dee doo dee . . . OK. Back already? That was pretty quick, but I'll take your word for it that you actually did go away and distract yourself after reading the stuff in italics up there.

If you've done it arightly, you're now fully acceptant of the concept of giving the damn things away as a method of acquiring 'em. For some folks, this one is a no-brainer. For others, the Zenness of it all is more than they can grok all at once. (Is "Zenness" a legal word? Dunno. Who cares—you get the idea.) And for some unfortunates, it's more than they can grok *ever*. Poor them.

You, dear reader, I shall presume to have sufficient mental horsepower to knead this one around in your head successfully.

Yes, It's True—the More You Give Away, the More You Get

Stop a minute here and think about it on a hard-assed practical level. With the business of giving computers away, only two things are required: input and output. The two of them add up to "throughput."

Once you've established any kind of *output*, a demand for *input* becomes necessary if you want to continue on your merry way with this. People understand this sort of thing without even *thinking* about it. You, oh kind soul, are going to rely on this understanding and exploit it.

Most folks are exceptionally kindhearted when given the *proper opportunity*. (Reread that and please note the Zenness contained within.) Everything boils down to setting up a situation where you can permit someone to display this kindheartedness at no risk to him or herself. And never underestimate the amount of risk someone can find in the business of being kindhearted. Tough guys hate it because it conflicts with their image. Liars and thieves don't like it because it makes them feel as if they're letting something slip through their fingers. Busy people don't like it because it takes away time from their ever-so-important lives. Even just plain folks are adverse to it. They worry that the word will get out on the street that they're pushovers. Nobody wants to be thought of as a pushover, do they? All of the above notwithstanding, everybody wants to believe that deep down inside they're a decent human being. It's just a matter of figuring out how to get them to express it.

Recruiting them as donors in your quest for free computers allows them all to grab off a little of that warm glow you get when you commit a kindness. Excepting full-blown psychopaths, everybody wants some of that warm glow once in a while.

Giving away free rigs for you to fix up and disperse allows them all the benefit with none of the drawbacks. It's just between you and them. (Learn how to suppress the urge to be a blabbermouth about the lives of your friends while you're at it here. The payoff will astound you.) They needn't worry about their image amongst the great swarm. You do all the work, including schlepping the damned crap out the front door and into your van, which allows them to remain sweat-free and clean of hand. You're also providing them with space (which there never seems to be enough of) to fill up with other, more important, detritus of life. And since a working computer is a gift that keeps on giving, they're allowed to occasionally sit back, sigh gently, and think nice thoughts about how they're enabling some poor, destitute college kid to grind out yet another term paper.

And so, you approach them in a fully nonthreatening manner and inquire after the status of any "dead" computers, computer parts, or whatever lurking in their closets, attics, basements, or sitting forlornly in plain view, unused.

You should not come across as anything except somebody who's interested in the greater welfare of us all. And if you cannot do this for whatever reason, then you can forget about it.

And let me stop right here for a minute and advise you that it's a good thing to be interested in the greater welfare of us all. With or without the damned computers, you're going to be an asset to your community, your friends, and yourself. Being nice does not mean that you have to roll over and play dead for every last schmuck that comes down the pike with a selfish agenda. Or *any* of them, for that matter. You are hereby authorized to defend yourself against idiots, greedy manipulators, guilt-trip pushers, control freaks, or any other denizens of the sideshow of human depravity. Screw 'em!

When you encounter any of these folks, hold firm to your own beliefs and don't let them sway you. And, while you're at it, perhaps advise them gently of the error of their ways. Sometimes they're being pricks through sheerest ignorance and nothing else. So go ahead and try to draw out of them whatever goodness may be hidden within.

Gets down off soapbox and wipes foam from around corners of mouth.

Alright, where were we?

Oh yeah. The book.

Why You Might Want to Help Your Fellow Human with Her Computer

Helping your fellow human with her computer directly helps you as well.

To begin with, it gets the word out on the street that you are someone with something going for them, i.e., a talent for fixing computers. That's a commodity, and not one to be undervalued. It's all give and take out there, and you had better be ready with a little something to give if you're looking forward to doing some taking. (And who isn't, in one way or another?)

Don't hurt none to have people regard you as kind and helpful, either. Additionally, it exposes you to a wider world of computer weirdness that you can tuck under your experience hat. Computer schooling is all well and good, but I can guarantee you that it will never teach you to check the printer cable for a couple of tiny pinpricks made by the needle-sharp teeth of the family kitten when you're troubleshooting that psychotically frustrating and intermittent (i.e., never happens when the repair guy is around) failure in a printer that you've taken home and repeatedly found to be rock solid and good as gold. Yep, that's a true story. I've got zillions of 'em.

And even if you can't fix the problem, you've still learned something. You now have an area of interest that you can pursue to broaden your knowledge. Since you're over at their house *just because you're a nice guy,* they're not going to cop an attitude over the fact that you failed to resolve their problem. There's always the $75-an-hour guy from the local computer fix-it place if you fail to come through for 'em. And the mere fact that you showed up and tried comes with special karma points that people *will* remember. Just be sure not to break anything while you're fumbling around.

And no, you don't have to work for free if you don't want to. You can charge everybody, nobody, or just some-body. It's entirely up to you. But keep in mind that while you're still learning the ropes here, you'll need to be extra careful about getting into situations over your head whilst plucking $20s out of somebody's wallet. The more you know, the better. And the less you charge (all the way down to and including nothing at all) the more that the folks you paid a visit to will be inclined to reimburse you in some other way. Don't be shy about your quest for free computers. Come right out and tell 'em. But be sure they understand that you're not in a hurry. I've had people give me free machines years later. See above, re: karma points and memory.

Upgrade Psychosis and You

Ahh . . . the joys of upgrade psychosis. We're living in a Golden Age here folks, in case you didn't know it. And since it can't last, my advice is to grab off as much as you can while the grabbing is good. Hmm . . . not a very Zenlike statement that, now is it? More contradictions. Oh well.

Were it not for upgrade psychosis, computers would be regarded more or less like some kind of toolbox full of sock-et sets, wrenches, and all that stuff. After all, a computer is merely a tool. But I know people who are in joyous, raptur-ous love with their computers. This I do not understand.

For me, a computer is just about as sexy as a pair of pliers. When I've got a nut that needs turning or something that needs a really strong grip to hold it, I whip out my trusty pair of pliers and put them to work, doing what it is that God intended for them to do. And when I'm done with the damn things, I put them right back where they belong and give them not a whit of further thought.

But computers are different; they're constantly morphing from one damn thing into another. Like all of a sudden, your pair of pliers needs electrical power. And then they need an extra handle. And then maybe a barometer. Followed by an absolutely essential subscription to *Cosmopolitan* magazine. Which is then chased down by . . . well, you're getting the idea here, yes? And when the morphing's done, whatever didn't make the latest greatest cut is abandoned. Does this make any sense at all?

Hell no!

The computers were doing just fine 10 years ago, and yet anybody with a 10-year-old computer is considered mildly, or perhaps massively, retarded. This, despite the fact that Old Reliable is still fully capable of churning out documents, crunching numbers, manipulating databases, calculating orbital elements for satellites, and all the rest of the jobs that this sort of tool is designed to perform.

But somehow, the great swarm has been persuaded that unless their machine has a set of bells and whistles that even Bill Gates wouldn't know how to make proper use of, then it's not worth having.

And, oh yeah, it's got to be able to run the latest operating system. Without the newest version of Windows, it's a piece of junk fit only for the landfill. And of course, since the software monopoly is thicker than thieves with the hardware monopoly, they're going to see to it that whatever they're trying to foist off on the public will not run on anything but the latest offerings of their megalomaniacal corporate brethren.

All of the above, while being too stupid to believe, is

nothing but good news for you and me, dear reader, because it means that there's a *massive* surplus of computers out there. Factories from Taiwan to Timbuktu are grinding them out by the millions, and great shoals of idiots in all 24 time zones are buying, buying, *buying* the damn things!

Pretty cool, huh?

It's like a little kid in some kind of Hitchcockian (or is that Twilight Zoneian?) toy store, unable to keep a grip on any one bauble because he's constantly distracted by an endless series of ever-more-attractive baubles, thus denying him the ability to properly enjoy any of it.

Serves him right.

YOU NEEDN'T WORRY IF THE DAMN THING COST YOU NOTHING

So OK. People are throwing computers away like there's no tomorrow. Which means, as you pluck the manna that falls from the sky onto the ground at your feet, that you have *nothing to lose.*

Pretty please read that one again and do like I said earlier about going off to distract yourself to let the fullness of *that* most very pregnant concept soak all the way through every last pore of your brain.

If you blow one of these babies clear to hell, no worries. There's gonna be another one coming down the pike here, real soon. Not only that, but the next one in the series will be better than the one before.

Try to start thinking of your free computers as a box of Kleenex. You can't get any use out of them unless you trash them. Use a computer. Toss it. Get another computer. Lather, rinse, repeat.

Once you've grokked this one properly, you've entered the freedom zone. You are free as a bird to do any damn thing you want to with your computer, up to and including filling it with potting soil and making a nice abode for your spider plants.

We're going to be churning through machines here, doing our best to bring them to life and give them away. We're not even going to keep the ones that work! So lose the anal attitude, OK?

In order to learn our craft, we must play around with the machines like a little kid taking a watch apart.

And so, when I start explaining to you what some doodad or other does, it's up to you to go grab your machine, take the cover off it, and dive in with gusto! Wheee! This is fun!

OK kiddies, here we go.

What's inside your computer.   Welcome mat.

Don't Be Afraid of Your Computer's Innards

Well then, whaddaya say we open the hood and have a look inside?

Ewwwwwww . . . . . . what *is* all that?

Not much, really. The main problem is all those damn *wires* snaking around all over the place, doing their best to make things look complicated.

Now try it without the wires.

Well then, that's not *nearly* as bad, is it? Almost looks like some kind of doormat. Which, in a very real way, it is. But instead of a doormat for people, it's a doormat for doo-dads. They all come together on the doormat and do their boogie, and the doormat keeps all the boogie in one place where it can do the most good.

Trust me on this one, there's nothing in here to be afraid of. Physically or mentally. These things are Lego sets. Legos are fairly easy to deal with, yes?

So don't be afraid.

Static Discharge in the Real World

While, yes, it IS true that static discharge (those sparks that zap you when you touch a doorknob on certain days) is capable of frying delicate electronic parts, the odds of this happening to you are far less than the wonks from engineering would have you believe.

On days when the doorknobs are biting, be sure and touch some little bare metal place (screw heads will do nicely if nothing else is available) on the case of your computer before you start grabbing the electronic diddywops within. Once you're seated in your chair working on the thing, you're pretty much no longer going to be generating static electricity unless you're weird and constantly rub the soles of your shoes back and forth on the carpet as you work. Since you're indoors, go ahead and take your stupid shoes off—they're 90 percent of the problem anyway. Bare feet ground quite well and don't permit static electricity to build up in your delightfully conductive body. On days when the humidity is low (take note, Arizonans), static electricity is worse than it is when the humidity is up there. Folks in Florida can ignore all worries about static discharge except for maybe three days in January.

When grabbing electrical pieces, try not to touch them on the shiny metal parts that are meant to conduct electricity into and out of them. Grab 'em by the edges if you have to. But since you've already touched the case of the computer and taken your shoes off, you really don't have to worry about it. And if I'm lying here and you do manage to cook something (it has never happened to me), don't worry. There's another free computer coming your way anyhow.

Pieces and Parts

OK, guys, let's talk about what a computer's made of. This one's easy—just three things: the box, the monitor, and the peripherals.

That's it.

Just three things. You can remember three things, can't you?

I knew you could.

The box is your computer. This is where we're going to be doing almost every last bit of our work.

The monitor is the TV thing that wires into the back of the box and lets you see a picture of whatever the hell your computer might be doing at any time.

The peripherals are anything else that connects to the back of the box (or, very rarely, the monitor).

If you've got a laptop, then the box, the monitor, and the peripherals are all one thing. Cool, huh?

Electrocution in the Real World

Alright dammit, these things do plug into the wall. And stuff that plugs into the wall can occasionally kill you. And since I told you that working in your bare feet, well-grounded to the floor, was not only fine and dandy but even *desirable,* I suppose I should give you a heads-up by way of

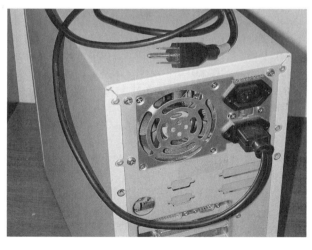

Here's your box. Serious electricity comes out of the wall, through that wire, and into your box.

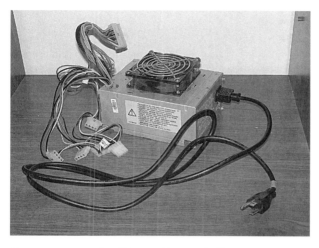

keeping a massive overload of electrons from coursing through your poor, conductive body, which was never designed to deal with such a weird possibility.

Your power supply, all by itself on a shelf.

The Box

Among other things, your box has a wire that comes out of its backside and heads directly to the closest power receptacle in your room.

Somewhere in there, there's the possibility of a good jolt, also known as your power supply. It's where the power comes from.

It HAS The Power.

Treat it with *utmost respect*.

If you're working on your computer while it's running (which you'll be doing a lot of the time), and you manage to spill beer in such a way that it forms a complete path between the innards of your power supply and yourself, YOUR POWER SUPPLY WILL ATTEMPT TO KILL YOU.

Do not let this happen, OK?

Your power supply is a touchy little beast possessed of a foul temper when prodded in an unkind way. Its temper is such that it may kill both you and itself in a fit of extreme spite.

And after they drag your dead carcass down to the local landfill, they'll still have to replace the damned power supply to get the computer working once again.

Your power supply hides in here

Danger lurks within, so be careful, OK?

Which is a shame.

The folks who design and build power supplies are well aware of these propensities. And so they shield them inside a metal box. The wonks from engineering will swear and declare that it's all in the name of RF shielding, but it also just happens to be the very best protection you can buy when it comes to preventing the introduction of an inadvertent elbow into the zone of death.

As if your power supply wasn't dangerous enough while plugged in to the wall, it's even dangerous as hell *when unplugged*. The damned thing has a MEMORY! It *remembers* the last dose of electricity that was fed into it for days and weeks. Years even, in certain unlucky cases. I'll talk about all that weirdness some more here in a little bit.

For now, it's enough that you treat your power supply with *utmost respect*.

The motherboard, cards, drives, and whatnot also live inside of the box. Excepting that thick, black wire that goes

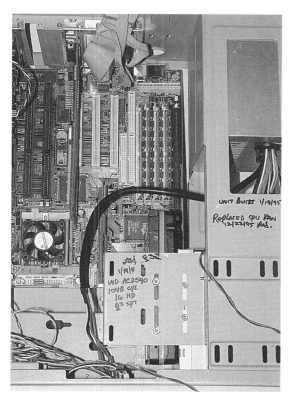

Except for the fat black wire that comes from your power supply, it's all as safe as mother's milk.

to your on/off switch, *none of this stuff can do anything to you.* It all runs on either 5 volts or 12 volts. For those of you who aren't aware, 12 volts is the exact same voltage as your car battery. (Car batteries, although possessed of a fine ability to generate big sparks, don't shock people; that's why automakers can leave the battery terminals exposed.) Needless to say, if 12 volts won't do it, then 5 volts won't do it either.

And that's the sum and total of your choice of voltages when poking around inside your box: 12 or 5, take your pick.

Which is not to say that it won't produce a nice "crack!" and a flash of blue light if you do something stupid while your machine is plugged in. Not at all. But one thing it *won't* do is shock you.

Which means you can play around in here to your little heart's content, with exactly zero chance of being bitten by bad electrons.

Tra la la!

The Monitor

Just stay out of this thing for the time being. It's not really part of your computer anyway; it's a separate thing that merely *attaches* to your computer to let you see what the hell's going on in there.

KEEP OUT!

Your monitor plugs directly into the wall and has its own power supply. Go back and read about power supplies, OK? DANGER.

But with a monitor, it's worse. Far, *far,* FAR *WORSE!*

The 115 volts (*more* than sufficient to kill you) that comes out of the wall socket would seem to be enough juice for anything, right? Wrong! Assuming your monitor has a big, fat picture tube just like your TV does, to properly operate it needs *tens of thousands of volts!* Flyback transformers are not your friends. (No, I'm not going to even tell you what a flyback transformer is.) And be assured that it's not the only thing inside your monitor that can kick you squarely into tomorrow's obituary page.

Just stay out of your monitor, OK?

And don't go spilling any beer on it, either.

Peripherals

Peripherals, being the uncertain sort of things they are, may or may not shock the living hell out of you.

As a rule of thumb, we'll work it this way: Anything that plugs into the wall with its own power cord is *verboten.* Anything without a power cord, that merely attaches directly to the back of the box or even *inside* the box, is fair game.

Some things can fall into either of the above categories,

depending on who made them and what they intend them to be doing. Speakers, for instance. Little rinky-dink speakers that sit on top of your box and merely plug into the back of it can be worked on with impunity. Big, honker megawatt subwoofer arrays that plug into the wall in addition to plugging into the back of the box should be left alone.

Once again:

1. Plugs into the wall: leave it alone!
2. Doesn't plug into the wall: dive in and have fun!

Chapter 2

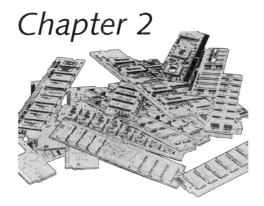

Places to Look for Freebies and How to Work Them

Well, alright. After all the foregoing you're probably wondering, "Where the hell are all these free computers, anyway? How come *I* don't have one?"

A fair question indeed.

So let's get down to some business here, shall we? The business of figuring out what kind of places you should be checking for free rigs, and perhaps how to work those places to ensure that the free rig becomes yours.

As a bit of introductory drivel, it helps to keep in mind that nearly everyplace has a computer, or 60, these days. Hell, if you're trying to get *away* from the infernal contraptions, it's almost impossible to do so.

This is good news.

Even better news is that computers are rendered obsolete at an incredible rate. You could not be living in a better time to be glomming onto free computers. Software and hardware are advancing by outrageous leaps and bounds. Monthly! When some new "killer app" comes along, there needs to be new machines to run the damned thing. When some new whizbang machine comes along, there needs to be new software created to take advantage of it. When the new stuff comes along, the old stuff has got to go!

This is just too cool to believe.

As long as we're not particularly interested in something akin to running a nested grid model for predicting the dynamics of worldwide weather into next season, or running some damned fancy new computer game, an old computer will work fine and dandy. (Don't get me started on what I think about computer games, except as a driving force for creating zillions of newly obsolete computers.)

It'll type your term paper *better* than the 100 teraflop Cray behemoth lurking behind the security apparatus down at the Lawrence Livermore lab. (This was written in 2002, before a 100 teraflop computer even exists. Care to place any bets as to how many months elapse before it sounds downright quaint?) It'll also get you on the Internet just as ticky-boo as you could ask for. Ditto playing a little music or any number of other neat-o things. Do not sell oldie-but-goodie rigs short—they are *powerful*. Even the decrepit ones. I'll leave it as an exercise for the student to determine how well her recently acquired Dumpster bomb stacks up against the computers that took Neil and the boys to the moon and back at the close of the '60s.

Going to the moon and back is not considered a trivial task. And if the computers they had back then could pull it off without leaving an interplanetary trail of dead bodies, then I'm guessing that what you have right now will do just fine.

COMPUTER STORES

Let's start looking for our free machine somewhere that might sound completely counterintuitive at first—let's go on down to the computer store and see what's shaking. You might be a little surprised by what you can find for free at a place that has dedicated its existence to *selling* you a computer.

But before we start searching, we need to know a little about what goes on in computer stores. And the main thing we need to know is that lots of computer stores do not just sell complete new systems out of a box, they also upgrade people's rigs. Especially the smaller, mom-and-pop kinds of places.

Every time a computer gets upgraded, there's going to be a fair bit of pieces and parts that get ripped out and replaced, giving the owner of the ripped-out pieces and parts a problem: what to do with this stuff? It takes up valuable space and it's not real flashy or new, and will therefore be more difficult to resell, even cheaply.

And so, the stuff starts accumulating on back shelves, growing ever less likely to justify its existence on that shelf with each passing month. Hard drives. Memory chips. Cases with power supplies. Motherboards. Floppy drives. CD drives. Ribbon cables. Oh hell, the list is endless. And no, right this minute you don't need to know a lick about what any of what I just wrote means. Just think of it as a room full of mumbo jumbo.

Anyhoo, it doesn't hurt one little bit to go into a computer store and ask the lady behind the counter (in the smaller shops she just might own the place) if you can "take out the trash." And stop right here and remember your social skills. If you look, sound, and smell like a homeless guy, she's gonna call the cops on you. You don't need a three-piece suit, but you do need to be presentable and have a nice manner about you. Voice tone is everything.

Also stop right here and take note of the slant to those words: take out the *trash*.

Don't be shy about letting them know that there might be something of some value in that pile of crap you'd like to help them get rid of. But just be sure that they know that you know that it's really just a bunch of junk.

This is going to be one of your major techniques for the duration of such time as you are looking for free computers (read: the rest of your life). You are looking for junk. Even if you are plainly aware of the value this stuff has, you must always act like it's junk. Rubbish. *Trash*.

Your aim is to present yourself as somebody doing them a favor! You are taking out their garbage—an onerous task that they would rather not have to spend the time and money to do themselves.

And keep in mind here that most of the stuff you schlep out of the back door of a computer store really *is* garbage. Completely useless for yourself and for anybody else. If there's a place where your free computer really isn't free, then this is it; you must put some sweat equity into the deal. When you've sifted through it all, the real junk must be dealt with. Go fill up somebody's Dumpster with it.

But, buried amongst the old 20 megabyte (MB) Seagate boat anchors, you'll almost always find a nugget or two. Perhaps a nice Pentium-equipped motherboard hiding inside a case that was proudly emblazoned with "386 16mhz" in big red letters on the front. Yep, I've found just exactly that. Ran it for a couple of years. Worked just fine. You don't need to know what 386 means right now. But when you finally do, you'll understand a little better about what I scored.

So go ahead and ask. If they say no, you haven't lost anything, have you? Nope.

And try to be driving a van or a pickup. You easily might get more than you bargained for. Some day I'll tell you about the Great Wall of Computers I dragged home from Symtek on Merritt Island. Jim Holsonback will back me up on that one.

WORK

Work is another place you can latch on to some good stuff. At least as long as you aren't one of the slacker bastards on the short list for a final visit to the assistant manager's office. Back to social skills again: You also need to be a good worker. Jesus, this stuff just won't go away, will it? Nope. It won't.

Anyhow, your workplace will have computers all over

the place. Unless maybe if you're a coconut-tree trimmer in Honolulu or something. Whatever.

Make friends with the boss, even if he's a total prick. Tell him that when it's time to replace the computers, you'll be glad to come in on your own time and help them—in exchange for *taking out the garbage*. Again. Same deal as at the computer store.

Bosses don't like to spend money on new equipment, so they're not going to be throwing out a whole raft of computers every week. Or even every year. But they do do it. They have to. And it's your job to be around when that happens.

Keep your eyes open. If you see a delivery guy walking through the back door pushing a cart loaded down with boxes of monitors, keyboards, and all the rest of it, ask somebody what's going on. "Hey, what are you gonna do with all that junk?" Maybe remind somebody that last spring, "Mr. Prickworthy told me I could take out the trash. Any trash in there?" You never know. Doesn't hurt to ask, and you might wind up with a windfall of working computers. Or at least a serious stash of spare parts.

Another angle at work consists in those female employees who would rather not have to lift and carry anything weighing more than 5 ounces. Look for high heels—usually a dead giveaway. If Miss Sniffy's monitor goes on the fritz, tell her you'll be glad to carry it out of the office for her and bring her back a new one from supply and put it on her desk for her. Once you've learned how to work with this stuff, you'll also be able to offer to plug it in and see if you can get it running. More favors. More social skills.

Ask somebody in charge if you can just take the "dead" monitor home. If they say yes, then do so. You can check it out later. I'll tell you a little bit about how later on in this thing.

This also gets you in touch with the folks in supply—a good thing. They've also got a lot of junk lying around. Volunteer to, yes, you guessed it, take out their trash. Just be sure to get the approval (written, if necessary) of whatever higher-up must pass judgment on it. When the leadership (especially if they're good Christian folk) is made aware of your "good works" in providing people (especially you) who couldn't otherwise afford them with free computers, your odds of being permitted to take out the trash skyrocket.

SCHOOL

School is kind of like work when it comes to computers. Except that work doesn't have a computer lab. Oh, heavenly computer labs—the promised land, where silicon manna falls from the sky into your lap! Actually, when it comes to electronic hardware, school isn't all that big of a deal. There's a horrendous bureaucracy associated with everything in a school, and computers loom large in the minds of paper pushers the world over. It's all entered into some damned ledger somewhere and it all has to be accounted for, disposed of properly using firm, fixed-price bidding, certified surplus material auctions, or some damn thing.

So unless you're just planning on *walking out the door* with the thing (happens all the time and nobody ever seems to notice, or even care), school isn't that well endowed with freebies.

Except for software.

Lotta software in school. Plus a lot of the lovely, small, thin, circular items that the software is stored on. Cases of them, in fact. And they can't possibly keep track of it all. Just load up and saunter on home.

School is the best place on the face of the Earth to grab software. The weenies in the computer lab spend two-thirds of their waking lives figuring out how to steal software and come up with the cracks to make it work. And after they've figured out how it works, they just can't keep it to themselves. What's the use in being a classroom hacker if you can't brag to all your buddies about your latest exploits in the realm of stolen software? And so, they share their stuff with all their pals. Maybe even you. Even if you're 50 years old and haven't seen the inside of a school since before Nixon was president.

Just watch out for viruses. Kiddies in computer labs are in love with viruses.

No, I really don't know why.

Just is.

FRIENDS AND FAMILY

Friends are another potential source of free computers—sometimes a complete, ready-to-use rig. I've captured more than just a few over the years this way. Do I need to get into your social skills again? No? Good. Glad to see that you're getting the picture here.

Put the word out to the entire crowd that you hang with that you're always on the lookout for computers. Dead or alive. Many times, dead computers contain an awful lot of live parts. We'll do more on that later.

If it turns out to be an old 8086 with a keyboard that's missing six keys and a black-and-white monitor that only shows words on the bottom half of the screen, take it anyway. Throw it in the garbage after you determine that there's nothing you can gain by keeping it. You're still ahead of the game. The friend whose computer/trash you were kind enough to take out, take home, and inspect to see if it could be recycled to a worthy recipient will remember what you did. And maybe tell one of his friends.

Whoo-wee. Now we're *networking*, baby! Welcome to the big time.

When you get good enough with computers to assist friends with their machines, things really start to take off.

People who can't plug the pieces together are *very* appreciative of someone who can. Especially if that someone is a good friend who takes the time to drop by and put everything back together after it was completely taken apart and moved out of the room to allow the new carpet to be installed. And so, they're going to be thinking of you when it comes to finding a good home for their dear old reliable (but now obsolete) machine. Ditto everybody else that they've told about your wonderful kindness.

Be good to your friends, even if they don't have computers or know anybody who does. It's just better that way.

Family is a lot like friends. Except that you don't get to pick and choose them. They're just there. Give 'em to understand that you're on a holy quest to spread computers far and wide across this great nation of ours, taking out the trash as you go. Fix their rigs when you can. One advantage to family is that they seem to be more susceptible to allowing guilt trips to be laid on them. All's fair in love and war. Just don't turn into some kind of manipulative bastard, OK? The computer's not worth it. Keep your karma as clean as you can.

CHURCH

Church is another great place to latch on to machines. Churches are ALWAYS looking for volunteers. This includes volunteering to work with the computers that the church deals with. Help them out with the stuff, even if it only means you loading the things onto a flatbed truck when their outreach mission is ready to send another hundred rigs to Bolivia.

Get to know the folks in the computer end of your church. Churches are magnets for free computers. There's tons of the stuff floating around sometimes. The folks in that end of the business are not always averse to seeing to it that some of the donated rigs stay close to home—real close to home. Maybe even *inside* their home. It's all part of the game and it's all pretty much understood, as long as nobody gets too flagrant about it.

Church is a good place to hook up with free computers even when you're a heathen dog, like me. After all, I really do give machines away to people. Without a doubt I have given away far more computers and computer parts than I have ever held on to. Church guys like that; once they discover I'm for real, they open up and are glad to help me with my little cause. And once in a while, I can return a favor or two. Nothing wrong with that, right?

DUMPSTERS AND THE SIDE OF THE ROAD

And we simply cannot forget the Great Roadside Computer Store. Kinda like the Great Roadside Furniture Store. You drive by on trash day, spot the junk, and then turn around and go back to get a closer look at it. Pluck whatever you want. No cover, no minimum.

Just last month (as I write these words) I spotted a couple of rigs in the grass in front of one of the houses in the subdivision here. Pulled over in the car, tossed 'em in the backseat, and drove home with 'em. Now mind you, this was in the morning following a heavy thunderstorm the night before, so I *just poured the water out* of the cases and monitors (no, I'm not joking here) and then let the stuff sit in the garage for a couple of days to dry out.

Net result: a worthless 386 that for some weird reason contained a perfectly good 56k (kilobyte) modem. The rig got tossed, but the modem now resides in my roommate's computer as a substantial upgrade to his old 33k modem. The second rig was a 486 in good working order with a 16-color monitor (that's really crappy). That said, it's going to a coworker shortly as a word processor for schoolwork along with an old dot-matrix printer (also really crappy) I had previously refused to throw away. All for nothing. Modem and word processor. Two very happy and appreciative people. And I learned a little something about computers and thunderstorms I didn't previously know. Neat-o, eh?

While we're at it here, don't forget your Dumpster-diving skills. Especially the Dumpster behind the computer store. And if there's any white-collar or high-tech businesses around with a Dumpster that isn't behind barbed wire, be sure and check that puppy on a regular basis too. Some of the stuff that comes out of Dumpsters is too cool to believe.

Another advantage to the side of the road, and Dumpsters, is that it's the only place where you won't need any social skills. So go right ahead and get really drunk and obnoxious if you'd like. The Dumpster won't mind a bit. As for the cop who watches you stagger back to your car with your booty and then swerve off into traffic, I can't really say.

This list of places to look for your new free computer is by no means exhaustive. The places to check are really only limited by your imagination, access, and social skills. Hell, when I was down at the bank cashing my pittance of a pay-check *this week* (as I write this), I casually tossed a remark to the teller asking what they did with their trash computers. Without so much as any further introductory claptrap, she leaned across and hit her supervisor with, "Do we own our computers or are they leased?" Right back came, "They're bought and paid for in full." The person who would know how they get disposed of wasn't in at the moment. I was told sweetly to ask again when I came back next week to cash the next paycheck.

(Author's note: The bank got bought out by another bank. What a surprise, eh? All the computers were replaced, but I didn't get any of the old ones. Some kind of bureaucratic thing. But I'm no worse off than I was before I asked. Can't win 'em all, but you won't win any of 'em if you fail to ask, ask, ask.)

Chapter 3

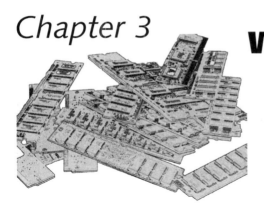

What Do I Do with This Pile of Junk?

OK. We now know what we're looking for. We know where to look for it. We know how to look for it. We know how to keep it from killing us as we work on it. And we know that our job is to build these things up from a semi-complete status until they work. And we finally know that once they're working, we're supposed to give them away.

As far as I can tell, all we really need to know at this point is how in the name of living hell are we supposed to work on them?

A lovely question. And one that I'm gonna start answering right now.

We'll start with tools. As in what you're going to need to work on a computer.

In many cases (pun intended) your entire tool kit will consist of one medium-size Phillips screwdriver.

Go find one on the side of the road or something. These things cost *nothing*.

Once in a while, your Phillips screwdriver won't do the job. Add a straight slot to the toolbox. Again, please go pluck this from off the ground someplace.

Should things get really hairy, you can drop a pair of

needle-nose pliers into that overloaded toolbox. Your uncle has a pair he hasn't used since Nixon was president. Go borrow his, long-term.

I've also made use of kitchen knives, mostly for prying apart stuff that's snapped together with damnable hidden latches. If the knife won't do it, the straight slot screwdriver certainly will. When attempting to straighten out a bent connector pin, I've found that a broken-in-half toothpick is sometimes just right for the job. Maybe go look around the local McDogfood's for your toothpick stash.

And finally, for you geezers with fading eyesight out there, sometimes a magnifying glass comes in mighty handy for reading eency-weency identification numbers off chips and things. You also might need it to make sure your teeny-tiny jumper is going onto the correct even teenier and tinier selector pins on the bottom of that old Seagate drive. Or perhaps a Maxtor. Some of these things have jumpers and pins that are just too small to believe; when you're working with them, they'll make you feel like Godzilla attempting to do brain surgery on a cockroach

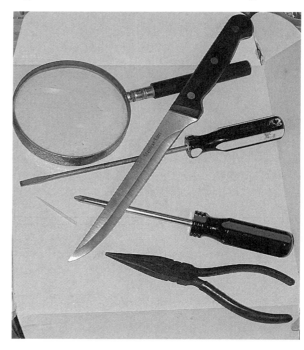

Deluxe tool kit.

using a pipe wrench and an anvil.

That's it for the tool kit. I've got lots of other tools, but I never use 'em on computers. Soldering irons, multimeters, crimpers, and all the rest of it just don't get used. Sometimes I think they're lonesome, languishing away in that unopened toolbox. Oh well.

Your grandma has more tools in the bottom of her purse, fer chrissakes.

Tools are a nonissue.

KEEP IT SIMPLE, STUPID

The first thing we're going to do with our free computer is to keep things simple. And the way we keep thing, simple is to work on one thing at a time, after which we test what we just worked on. This keeps us from getting confused.

If we drop in a stick of memory, put a modem and a video card into the slots on the motherboard, and hook up a pair of hard drives along with a CD-ROM, the machine stands an excellent chance of not working when we power it up. Which part was the culprit? Dunno. Trust me here, you'll never figure it out if this happens to you.

Oftentimes, all of the new parts we put into the machine work fine separately, but owing to the cussedness of computers, they will refuse to work in the presence of one another.

So what we do is make sure that things like monitors, keyboards, and mouses (the big three) are proven good before we go hooking up that new machine to them. That way, we should be able to communicate with our machine when we plug it in. Of the three, the monitor is most crucial. If you don't get some kind of screen, with some kind of information (no matter how cryptic) on it, you're dead.

Fortunately, most monitors will work, more or less, with most computers. If the plugs fit together, you're probably alright.

Ditto keyboards and meeses.

This is your whole computer (I told you it was simple).

Of the three objects, the only one that you can do without in a major pinch would be the furry vermin. Keyboard and monitor are *absolutely essential*.

Once we're in business with the big three, we can proceed to check out the machine.

One thing at a time!

INSIDE THE BOX

Your machine(s) will doubtless look different than the computer shown above in some ways, but the basic guts will not change. Ever. Sometimes I think computer manufacturers make things look complicated so they can impress you with their wonderfully intricate gizmos in order to charge you more, more, more.

The motherboard is powered by the power supply. The big three plug into the motherboard or cards that go into those slots on the motherboard. And that's it!

On the motherboard lives the CPU (your computer's brain). Most of the time it has its own socket that it can be removed from, but once in a while you'll find the CPU soldered down, unremoveable. Ditto memory. Don't matter, either way.

And that's it!

Anything else is, by definition, a peripheral. Which, we'll shortly discover, is what doesn't work nine times out of 10 when dealing with "broken" computers.

The Case

Whaddaya say we talk about the thing that makes your box a box? As in the metal case itself—the container for all the rest of that stuff.

There's a few tidbits here that don't properly live inside the box and sometimes they can go bad. On/off switches for instance. Before you tear the whole damned thing apart 'cause it won't do anything when you press the button, you might wanna have a look at the button itself—but be careful of the on/off button, OK? Sometimes it's connected *directly* to the power supply with a fat black wire, which carries the full wallop that comes out of your wall socket. Disconnect the machine from the wall socket before attempting to discover problems with the on/off switch. But sometimes, that's the whole deal right there—fix the switch and you've got a perfectly fine computer on your hands all of a sudden.

Don't plan on getting this lucky very often; it does happen, just not very much.

If you can't figure out how to fix the switch, grab one of the spare power supplies you have lying around and replace the whole damned power supply and be done with it. More on this in a bit.

Turbo switches are a laugh and can be ignored for the most part; we'll see them again here in a little while too. Reset switches are quite a bit more useful but can still be done without. If you can, track the wires (occasionally a Herculean task, not worth the aggravation it causes) from "turbo" and "reset" to the little pins on the motherboard. If the wires aren't there to begin with, sometimes you get lucky and right next to the pins on the motherboard will be the words "turbo" and "reset." Short across 'em with a screwdriver (machine plugged in and running) to see if they do anything. If they're working, you might wanna keep the little wires hooked up to 'em so that when you press the button on the case, it actually does something.

Other things on the case, like lights and tinny little speakers, can be ignored for the most part. I have yet to encounter a box that won't work 'cause the blinkenlights on the case were dead.

When given free computers, sometimes you'll find that it's just the case and power supply. Snatch the power supply out of there immediately and save it (see above). Maybe save the case too. Sometimes you get things like bare motherboards that will need a case to live inside of, but cases are horrid space wasters. Keep the best one or two and ditch the rest unless you're living in the loft area of a converted barn and have LOTS of room downstairs.

And while we're at it here, with tools in hand, I guess this is where I need to tell you to save all them weirdie little screws and fasteners that hold stuff together. Some of 'em are just as non-standard as can be and if you ever need one and don't have it, you're in trouble. Save that crap in baby food jars or something, OK?

Bailed out by a spare part.

The Power Supply

So alright then, whaddaya say we revisit the power supply? Now that we know that it can do us great bodily harm and are therefore sufficiently careful and cautious, I suppose we can work on it. And, as it turns out, there's very little work to do on a power supply.

Take the metal case off the power supply, being *especially careful* not to touch the contacts underneath the filter condensers. The filter condensers are *capacitors,* which are sort of like batteries in that they hold a charge. Most of the capacitors in your computer are teeny little things that would have trouble hurting a fly—except for inside the power supply. Filter condensers take current directly out of the wall plug and sort of hold on to it. You can't see it, but it's still in there. And if you bump against the contacts on the bottoms of these things, the full wallop will come sparking out of there and knock the living hell out of you!

Capacitors in general look like little cans. The filter condensers will be the biggest cans. Stay away from can-looking things in general. You can't do a damn thing to make them better, and *they* have ways to make *you* worse. (You folks who know how to check and replace caps have no business reading this part of the book. You already know more than what I'm sharing with the other folks. Go read the part about social skills—you need it, trust me.) The contacts for the filter condensers will almost always be on the other side of the printed circuit board that they're living on. Look for a pair of soldered wire nubs sticking through the printed circuit board exactly on the other side from the big cans and *stay away from 'em.*

Back during my electronics shop days in high school, we'd play "think fast" with live filter condensers—just throw them at somebody when they weren't looking and holler "THINK FAST!" Even people who had endured this already (a club all of us joined sooner instead of later) would invariably put a hand up to deflect the object flying their way. *ZAP!* Nobody got killed or anything, but I strongly recommend against trying this stuff with someone. They might not get the joke and come over and simply knock your teeth down your throat. Or wait patiently to get you in some other way weeks later. You have been warned.

If the power supply's completely dead and won't send power anywhere, have a look around for any glass fuses and check to see if any of 'em are blown. (No, they're not always there, and if there's no fuse, you're outta luck with this one.) If the fuse is blown, the little wire inside the glass tube will have a break in it and won't go continuously from one side of the fuse to the other. Hopefully, the fuse will have sufficient identification on it somewhere to allow you to replace it with the correct fuse. Don't just throw any old fuse in there: bad things could result.

The only sensible thing that you can do any good with inside the power supply is the fan. Fans, being mechanical deals with moving parts, tend to fail more often than the rest of this stuff. You can easily tell if the fan in your power supply (or any other fan for that matter) is no good any more. A bad fan, with the power turned on and your machine otherwise happily running, won't be turning. Or perhaps it will be turning slowly and making an unpleasant noise, which is anything other than a soft whirrrrr and the sound of air moving. Or no sound whatsoever, despite a see-through blur of obviously whirling blades. If you leave the fan on a power supply in a broken state of nonturning uselessness, your power supply will eventually overheat and die. My latest power supply to do that was, as usual, possessed of a weird-ass fan that used weird-ass voltage, and I never did find a matching replacement. Took about four months (I run all my computers without the cases on them, giving the computer plenty of additional ventilation and me plenty of additional RF), but sure enough, one fine day the computer no longer turned on when I hit the switch. At which point I grabbed one of my spares off the shelf and replaced the dead one with it and I'm still running fine, even as I type these words.

So there's the deal with power supplies: Replace the fuse, replace the fan, or just replace the whole power supply and be done with it. Whatever suits you.

The Motherboard

Alright then, back to the doormat. If your computer were the Pentagon, this would be the E Ring, where all the generals and admirals hang out with their flunkies. And, as with generals and admirals, you can't really *do* anything with your motherboard. Your only real option is the same one that Truman had with MacArthur: When your motherboard begins to act strangely or becomes insubordinate, you simply get rid of it.

You'll know your motherboard is the culprit only after you have eliminated every other component in your

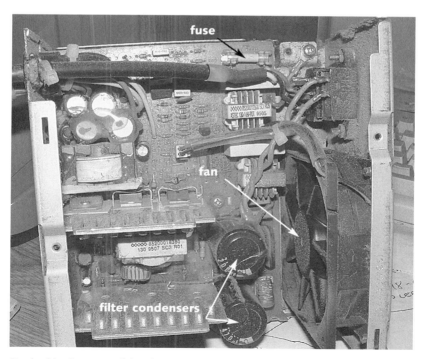

Be double damn careful in here, OK?

machine as a possible source of the distemper (including power supplies, which can produce some spectacularly weird effects if the voltages they're supplying to the motherboard get squirrelly). Motherboards hardly ever break without some kind of cruel mistreatment from owners or users. Keep the beer out of the computer and you can expect your motherboard to hum along happily far into an age where it has become laughably obsolete.

And before all of you Slashdot, codeheaded, techno-weenie bastards start in with "inspect and replace bad caps" and anything else along those lines, just knock it off, OK? First of all, that sort of thing is not, and never was, intended to lie within the scope of this book. The title of this book is not *Advanced Technical Diagnostics and Repair Techniques for Case Modders, Overclockers, and Other Idiots Utterly Lacking in Any Kind of Social Skills*. Second of all, this is *my* book. If you don't like my book, I suggest you go

Brain salad sandwich: CPU fan on top, heat sink in middle, CPU (hidden) below heat sink, CPU socket on motherboard at bottom.

write your own book. And after you write it, see if you can sell it. Best of luck.

Now, where were we? Oh yeah, motherboards.

While the board itself is unworkable, it does contain a few doodads that you *can* work with.

Let's go look at some of that stuff.

The CPU

Please introduce yourself to your computer's brain, the CPU. That's Central Processing Unit for those who can't stand it when undefined acronyms swim by.

Sometimes your CPU lives in a socket, lying flat on the motherboard. Sometimes it's inside a metal thingamajig, hidden from sight and placed edge down into the motherboard. Once in a while, it's soldered down and there's not a damn thing you can do with it. It's also supposed to always have a heat sink and fan on it (unless it's an old 386, which will only be good to run DOS stuff and serve as a word processor to do term papers with). Sometimes, when dealing with heat sinks and fans, people hang on to 'em and give you the computer without 'em.

With plenty of ventilation, your CPU may survive without out benefit of a fan, but probably not. Without the heat sink, forget it. Just for fun, undo the weirdie little clip thing(s) and take that crap off your CPU (mind the thermal grease and don't make a

CPUs and associated junk-ola.

big mess) and fire your machine up and let it run for oh,
say 10 seconds. Now put your finger on top of the CPU.
Ouch! Damn, that thing gets HOT! Now go turn your
machine off before it self-destructs.

And overheating is just about the only way to toast your
CPU, except for lightning strikes, beer spills, and that sort of
thing. CPUs last essentially forever, which is good 'cause
you can't do anything to fix 'em. They either work or they
don't work.

After you've been doing this a while, you will learn how
to replace CPUs, but I'm not sure if I want to get into that
with you right now. Mainly it boils down to making sure
that the speed of your CPU is more or less matched to what
the motherboard wants to run at (we'll hit that again here
in a bit) and being sure to match voltages between CPU and
the socket it goes into.

A good reason to keep some spare motherboards around
is so you can check to see if the CPU on your latest non-
working acquisition is the source of the problem.

A word on CPU nomenclature: For our purposes (go
away, Mac people—this isn't for you) the original processor
was something called an 8080. (This was back when everybody wore loincloths and hunted mastodons using rocks
and clubs.) After that came the 286 and then the 386 followed by the 486, at which point the folks at Intel decided
that attempting to copyright a *number* wasn't such a good
idea after all and so they came up with the name Pentium.
And then it went Pentium 1, Pentium 2, etc. I don't even
know where they are with it right now. I think they've
decided to come up with all new names. As this was going
on, AMD (the other major CPU manufacturer) was pooting
along with –86 kinds of names and after that went to K
things. We got up to K–8 or some damned thing, and now I
think that bunch, too, has decided to swamp us with a host
of new individual names.

What I just told you is deliberately distorted, missing a
few vital bits of information, and is generally of little use in

the real world. Bottom line, none of this matters. What you should really be paying attention to is your CPU's *speed*.

CPU speed is measured in hertz. Don't ask. I never met the guy and personally, I still prefer cycles per second. Anyhoo, the more hertz, the better. And it's not enough to simply know that 600 is a bigger number than 3. You also need to be able to tell your megas from your gigas. One giga is worth a thousand megas—pretty good rate of exchange, eh?

Anything below about 100 megahertz isn't gonna cut it anymore. It won't run any worthwhile software anymore (thank you, Microsoft, for that little favor). Which means, excepting primitivo rigs fit only for college term paper production, 486s and below are useless. They just don't run fast enough. *Sigh.*

I'll tell you how to check your CPU's speed later on.

Keep in mind that with each passing year after this is being written (2003), the bar will get raised a little higher. While this is good in that it provides us with an endless supply of free computers, it's bad in that it makes the whole damned subject a moving target. You've gotta just keep up with it, OK? If this thing sells, I'll update as required in the second edition. If it bombs, you're on your own.

Now we come to the CPU fan.

Oh joy, another *mechanical* diddybop. As in something that stands a much higher chance of breaking owing to its being composed of moving things that rub against one another.

Your CPU fan is clipped or screwed or integrally built into the heat sink that lives on top of your CPU. It's a cute little thing, perhaps the size of a silver dollar, perhaps a bit larger, but don't let its insignificant size fool you. A broken CPU fan will invariably result in a broken CPU, and oftentimes it's sooner instead of later. Worse, it's buried way the hell up inside of your rig, and if it just dies without so much as a pre-emptory clunk or whine, you won't know anything happened at all until your computer has a cerebral thrombosis when the CPU overheats.

Once in a peculiarly shaded moon of blue, the CPU overheating won't actually kill the CPU but will give it a case of temporary schizophrenia. The machine's owner will think it's gone to computer heaven and give it away to you. When you open it up to have a look around inside, you'll discover a dead CPU fan and replace it. Suddenly you have a perfectly good computer on your hands. Yes, it happens. No, not very often.

CPU fans can plug into the octopus tentacles reaching out from your power supply, or they can plug in somewhere on the motherboard. Be sure the damned thing is plugged in, OK?

CPU fans almost always come with a round sticker glued to the hub, with some identification mumbo jumbo on it. Screw the mumbo jumbo and remove the sticker. Underneath, hidden away from prying eyes (computer manufacturers just love to hide stuff under stickers), will be the central bearing. If the CPU fan is running slowly, intermittently, making a loud buzzing sound, or perhaps all of the above, sometimes a drop of oil on that bearing will clear everything right up. (Read that again: one drop. No more. And make that a small drop while you're at it.) Or not. Or just for a while, and you'll have to repeat this step as many times as you have to. Occasionally the bearing is gummed up with the crust that adheres to the innards of older computers and the drop will need to be rubbing alcohol instead. Cleans off the crust. It's worth a try, anyway. CPU fans are pesty to come by for some reason. People like to hang on to 'em.

All this hoo-ha about some damned fan buried down inside the catacombs of your computer is yet another reason to run your rig without a case. Everything is right there in (more or less) plain sight. With the case off, you can spot silliness like this before it bites you on the ass. RF paranoics will just have to put on a few extra layers of foil on their AFDB to ward off the evil effects of invisible waves propagating their way from inside their computers.

Jumpers

Jumpers. Gack. One of my least favorite subjects. Mystery pins.

And motherboards (and almost everything else too) just bristle with the things. Like cactuses.

Sometimes, you're just as lucky as hell and your motherboard will have every last jumper clearly labeled as to its precise function. Most of the time though, you're just dealing with a generic cactus and have no clue as to what it's all for.

Now that I think about it, jumpers are such an obnox-

Downtown, on the corner of Jumpers and Main.

ious subject that I'm gonna talk about something else here for a little while. It's sorta related to jumpers, but it also relates to a whole slew of other things too. It's the business of having to go to the Internet to get information on things like jumper settings.

No two motherboards are alike when it comes to jumpers—even if they are the same model from the same company! I dunno, it's almost like the manufacturers are playing a little game with us here, just to see if we can figure this arcane garbage out. And so, you have to go to the Internet for your information. Hopefully, you'll find a site that's run by the people who made the infernal contraption in question, but that's not always the case. Lots of things can happen: they go out of business; they get bought by some other company and you can't find the old name and don't know the new one; they just didn't feel like taking the time and money to put a proper Web site up; or their Web site is "temporarily" down (like for the last seven months and counting). Who knows?

And if that happens, you've gotta start wading through all the newsgroups, bulletin boards, "support" groups, and glancing references to your mystery board as you may obtain on the World Wide Wilderness. This information is constantly shimmering, flickering, morphing from one damned thing into another, and just refusing to remain in existence for any extended period of time.

You start out by going to Google and punching in what pittance of information may be cryptically printed on your motherboard. (Google is our preferred search engine as of the printing of this thing. Go check the copyright notice, OK?)

And then you just sort of go from there, following an endless branching labyrinth of paths that probably don't lead anywhere useful, but that must be kept track of (save them URLs!) by copying stuff to Notepad or bare-handing it onto paper with an actual pen or pencil. If you don't keep track of this stuff, you will wind up (almost always sooner instead of later) wanting to go back to one of 'em to dig a little further and won't ever again in your life able to find it. Poof, and it's gone!

And so, my little section on jumpers is really a section on finding technical information on the Internet. Which means that you'd better be equipped with a functioning computer to do this stuff while you work on the nonfunctioning computer lying in pieces all over the place. While it's true that the computers down at the local library will work just fine, they're not right there in your workspace, ultrahandy for checking things that pop up unannounced *right now*! Something certainly is better than nothing, but see if you can get a working Internet connection right next to the machine you're working on. You'll be glad you did. Especially when it comes to drivers for weirdie hardware.

All of this means that you'd better be equipped with a functioning ability to search the Web for information. If you're not really any good at this, then now is the time to start learning! Not tomorrow, not next week, but now. Put this book down right this second and go look up something weird and arcane on the Web. Perhaps Dutch tulip prices in 1636. Or maybe what the Mercury space capsule that Alan Shepard flew in was made out of. See just how much you can dig up. If you encounter weirdness that you don't really understand (the bizarre world of newsgroups perhaps?), then make a note of it and go research that too!

Jumpers are the simplest things in the world to manipulate, once you know the proper settings. Just grab the needle-nose pliers (hell, tweezers will work fine and dandy too), pluck the little jumper doodad off one pair of pins, move it to some other pair of pins, and—hey, presto!—you're in business.

Fortunately for you, most motherboards are already okey and dokey in "as is" condition when it comes to jumpers; it's pretty rare to have to reset jumpers to make one go. But, people like to fiddle around with their machines, and if they don't know what the hell they're doing, they just might move a jumper around and then not remember doing it or where it originally came from. This, I've seen with my own eyes. Sometimes your machine is one jumper setting away from perfect working condition.

So ya gotta know where the damn jumpers belong in the first place. If "J23" needs to be jumped across pins 1–2 and it's sitting there on pins 2–3, you need to be able to sort this out.

Needless to say, if the motherboard is already working happily, stay away from the jumpers, OK?

Cables

You would think that something as simple as *wires* wouldn't be a problem, yes?

No.

Wires gotta do two things for your machine to work. First, they've gotta work themselves. Second, they've gotta be plugged in to the right thing, the right way.

The second problem is easiest to deal with, so let's hit it first. In general, the people who made your computer tried their best to fix things so that you can't hook up the wires the wrong way. Each one of the wires going to your computer or living inside your computer is more or less an individual. Each has a particular shape and has a particularly shaped socket that it plugs into. And if that's not enough help, they also have plugs and sockets that only go together one way.

But not *always*.

The very worst offenders seem to be floppy-disk drives. Sometimes there's a little key thing on either the cable or the socket on the back of the floppy drive to

The shape of the thing forces you to put the right plug in the right hole the right way.

force things to fit correctly or not fit at all. Sometimes there's just a little *shaded area* on the cable where the little key thing oughtta be to kind of tell you what should be happening, but isn't. Sometimes there's a little notch in the printed circuit board that the socket lives on that pretends to be waiting to accept the key on the cable plug. You would think that with all these precautions that floppy cables would be no problem to get right. Think again. I have seen floppy drives where the little key thing on the wire fit all the way on the opposite side from the little notch on the printed circuit board!

Bottom line: If the light on your floppy drive comes on at bootup and never goes off and your floppy drive won't work, turn the cable around the other way—it's hooked up backward. Happens all the time.

Ribbon cables (that's what goes to floppies and hard drives) are fairly anonymous-looking things, but if you take a close look, you'll discover that one side or the other has some marks, or maybe some red color, on one edge of the cable but not the other. This is the Pin 1 side of the cable. If the socket that it goes into on the motherboard, or wherever, isn't keyed, look for a teeny, tiny "1" or "2" at one end of the socket pins. Do I need to tell you that if you see a "48" then you can assume that the "1" is on the other end? God, I hope not. Match the marked side of the ribbon cable with the side of the socket plugs marked "1" or "2." Once in a while the socket pins on a floppy or a hard drive will have that little 1 or 2. Same deal as with the motherboard. Match 'em up. If it's

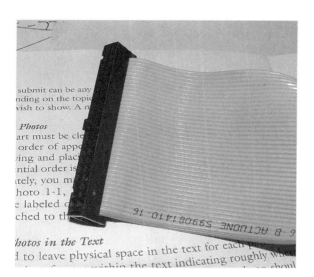

The key keeps it from going in backward and if that's not enough, the writing and red line down one edge are always on the Pin 1 edge of the cable.

just impossible to tell, then go ahead and hook the damn thing up any whichaway. Even if it's backward it won't fry anything. If it doesn't work, reverse the cable on one end and try it again. If it still doesn't work, you either have a bad drive, a bad motherboard, or a bad cable.

Mind how the power-supply cables hook to the mother- board. Sometimes it's a split connector and each half can be switched for the other. If things are lying around loose, be sure to fix it so that the black wires on each half of the split connector are *adjacent* to each other when you're plugged in.

Have some spare cables lying around. Once they've been checked as working, mark 'em as such and date 'em too. When in doubt about something, swap the cable to see if that's the source of your trouble. Cables go bad more often than you might imagine. And, while we're at it here, check those "good" cables in your stash (using a working machine with working parts) every so often. How they go bad just lying in a bag is beyond me, but I've seen it hap- pen. Dunno how, just does.

Sometimes the back of your machine will have more than one socket to accept the same kind of wire. Sometimes both sockets will work just fine (especially so when it's USB sockets). Usually though, they won't. Mark the one that works and leave the other one alone. Open up the machine and see if the dead one even has wires going to it inside the machine. If not, you can remove the sock- et—less confusion that way. Later on, if you get that spe- cial cable that hooks it up inside the machine (and you fig- ure out how to do it and why to do it), then just put it back on. Needless to say, you did not throw it away when you removed it, yes?

One way to check a suspicious cable is to wiggle it right next to where the wire part becomes the plug part, with the machine plugged in and running. This is where wires fail. If your hardware gets squirrelly when you do this, then the odds are good that it's the wire that's causing the problem.

This happens quite often with intermittent problems that are impossible to reproduce.

Bottom line: Check the wire!

Expansion Slots

Alrighty, here's where you can really have some fun just goofing around with things: The expansion slots. Nothing actually *expands* here, but things do get added. Maybe they should have called 'em adder slots. And put a picture of a really neat snake next to 'em. Yeah, that's it!

Never mind.

Yet another bottom line is: If it fits in the expansion slot, then go ahead and plug it in! Whee, this is fun! Of course, be sure and do this stuff when the machine is turned off. You'll fry it for sure if you attempt to plug or unplug while your rig is hot.

Expansion slots come in a variety of flavors, each with their own name. Nope, not gonna tell ya what the names are. If the thing you're doodling around with fits into the slot, that's all you'll ever need to know about what kind of slot it is. No need in cluttering up our minds with arcane trivia, is there?

Slot machine.

On the back of your computer, there's a whole series of metal strip-looking things that cover the holes available for the cards that drop into the slots. You have to remove one of the strips to allow the socket(s) on the card to show itself to the outside world in order to plug wires into it. Mostly the strips are attached with a Phillips screw on the top. Sometimes they just kind of snap into place. Sometimes, on proprietary machines (often found as leftovers from some business or other), the slot covers are still kind of attached to the case of the machine and you have to wiggle them back and forth and kind of break them off at the bottom to expose the slot in the back of the case. Regardless of how

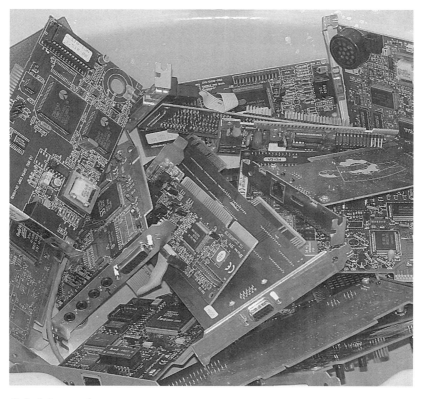

Sink-full-o-cards.

it's done, you gotta have that exposed hole/slot showing before you go dropping cards into your expansion slots.

Cards

Well then, here's one of the main events: cards. Cards are what go into your expansion slots.

In the ancient days of yore, everything had its own card that had to be dropped into a slot. Modems, drive controllers, printer cards, sound cards, game cards, video cards, LAN cards, hell, just about everything except the ace of spades.

Nowadays, the folks who make the motherboards have figured out that everybody needs a modem, LAN connection, game port, drive controllers, sound connection, video connection (duh!), USB ports, printers, and a never-ending list of other goodies as they become widely available. And so now they're just building this stuff right in to the motherboards—sometimes some of it, sometimes all of it, but never none of it. But the older the motherboard you're dealing with, the less of this stuff is going to be built in.

And the stuff that's not built in is gonna have to be handled by cards.

So you're gonna be dealing with cards.

Cards can be the most annoying things you'll ever encounter in your life. They can also work perfectly from the git-go, without so much as a crooked fart.

You just never know until you plug the damned thing in and see if what attaches to it lights up and works as specified.

I'm not gonna talk about every last kind of card that you might stumble across, and (for that matter) a lot of the ones you'll see every day too. LAN cards for instance. If you're considering hooking up a Local Area Network, then what are you doing reading *this* book? You already know all this stuff. Go away!

Modems

Gotta have a modem. How the hell you gonna get on

the Internet without a modem? I haven't yet figured out how to get Internet access for free via high-speed cable connection, and therefore will not talk about it in this book. Ditto wifi. Should this thing go into a

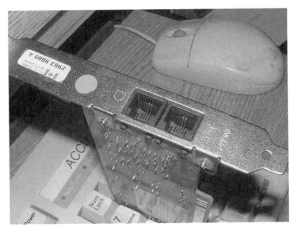

Business end of a modem.

second printing, I'm pretty sure that both of these subjects will be covered, thank you very much. But not now. Maybe some kind soul will share the secret of free high-speed Internet with me. I'm all ears, in case anybody is out there with a plan that works. Having a roommate with a DSL line who lets you use her connection is *not* a plan that works, by the way. Remember, guys, not only the connection itself but the hardware must be free, free, free.

Why Modems Suck

I hate modems. And the older the machine, modem, and operating system, the more I hate them. Modems are the great nonstandard item.

And they're fussy little bitches too. One wrong word, and BANG! Forget about it.

Modems work with things like IRQs and "interrupts." Mostly what gets interrupted is your pleasant afternoon as you gnash your teeth in rage as the thing refuses to work like it's supposed to.

Proprietary boxes (Compaq, Dell, Gateway, eMachine, that kind of crap) oftentimes come with proprietary modems. The damnable things will not work in somebody else's box. Linux HATES Winmodems. Here are some reasons why I hate modems:

1. Your modem will vie for control of com1 with your serial mouse and both will refuse to work.
2. Your modem will have some godawful concatenation of jumper settings required and no instructions on how to set it.
3. Your modem will require device drivers that your operating system has never heard of and will not run.
4. Your operating system won't have the correct device driver for your modem and you'll discover that nobody in the known universe does either.
5. Your modem will work just fine and dandy in machine "A" but will utterly refuse to light up in machine "B" despite machine A and B both running all the same software otherwise.
6. Your operating system (especially operating systems with names that end in two digits, the first of which is a "9") will be utterly unable to even discover that you have a modem plugged into the machine.
7. Your modem will fail to work the first three times you try it, and then *for no reason whatsoever* will crank right up on the fourth boot.
8. Your modem will lie to your operating system and try to tell it that it's something that it's not. Your operating system will be understandably confused and will endlessly attempt to load the wrong device drivers for your lying modem.

Are we getting the idea here yet? I sure hope so.

Of all the crap I've ever spent time fighting with in an attempt to get the thing to *please* run in some machine, everything else put together doesn't add up to the time spent on modems. They're THAT bad.

They're getting better nowadays, but since we're dealing with cast-off machines and equipment, that's of little solace.

Farting around with modems will teach you all the gory details of your "device manager." Your device manager is an evil thing, fully capable of wrecking your entire system if mishandled. Treat it with care. Evil or not, you must learn how to putz around in here in order to persuade recalcitrant hardware to obey your orders.

Because of modems, I became familiar with my device manager, and it's probably where you're going to become familiar with it too. If you don't know where it lives, just go to your help screen and type in "device manager" in that index-box thing. Different versions of Windoze sometimes keep it in different places. I guess Bill Gates likes playing hide-and-seek. I dunno. But like I said just a minute ago, BE CAREFUL in there. You go pooting around mindlessly, and all of a sudden you're reloading your entire operating system from scratch.

If your modem isn't responding, or is giving error messages, or is just being a pain, go into the device manager and simply eradicate it. Your computer will give you alarming messages advising you not to do this but since the modem's not working anyway, why not? Rip it out by the roots. Then reboot your machine and see what happens. Sometimes it will discover the modem. Sometimes you'll have to tell it a little about your modem. Sometimes it gets coy and refuses to tell you the whole story, which you'll have to figure out for yourself and then tell the stupid machine. Sometimes you'll have to pick a modem from a list the computer hands you. Sometimes your exact modem isn't on the damned list. Sometimes you can fudge by picking a different modem off the list and the frickin' thing will actually spin right up and work! Sometimes you're just outta luck. Sometimes you can search the Internet for your modem and download a file called a "device driver" file, follow the instructions you find in it, and *that* will work. Or not.

If you think your modem is working but would like more information before attempting to dial up AOL, go to your control panel and invoke "modems" (or "phone and modem options," or whatever the damned thing is calling it these days). Poke around in the submenus until you find something called "diagnostics" and then invoke that, being careful to ensure that the particular COMM port where the damnable modem is supposed to be lurking is highlighted. Give it a few seconds, and if the modem is OK, then you'll get a bunch of gobbledygook in that little open box. Hopefully, amongst cryptic crap like "S00 = 000 S01 = 000" and Bob knows what else, you'll see perhaps your modem's name, or the word "success" or something that looks to be some sort of vague English. Generally speaking, if you get a bunch of words and numbers, it's a good thing. The machine has to actually find and talk to your modem to generate this stuff.

Keep in mind that if you don't have an installation CD, you might be completely out of luck. Installation CDs are golden. Grab 'em every chance you get. Multiple copies of a Windows95 installation CD might seem to be a bit silly to keep around, but I've discovered that every once in a while you'll not only need one of the damned things, you'll need more than one. No, I'm not going to belabor the issue by giving you all the precise details of exactly how this might come to pass. Just trust me here, OK?

Talk of installation CDs leads directly to talk of CD drives. As in, if you don't have one, nothing at all is going to happen with your installation CD. And you thought we were doing this section on *modems*, didn't you?

And now we've discovered yet another reason why modems suck. They almost always *demand* a functioning CD drive and Windoze installation disk. Without this pair of jewels, you're outta luck, buckaroo.

Something else here, while we're at it, whaddaya say? Dating your equipment by reading the little numbers off the chips on the cards.

Most chips have strings of numbers on them. You might need to whip out your trusty magnifying glass to read the

That little "9932" is telling you this Conexant chip was manufactured in the 32nd week of the year 1999.

little peckers, but they're there. Among the mysterious numbers are oftentimes four-digit jobs that tell you when your doodad was manufactured. The first two digits are the last two digits of the year (99 stands for 1999), and the second two are the week number of the year. Needless to say, four-digit number strings with numbers like 3389 can be ignored because they weren't making computer chips in the 89th week of the year 1933.

Computers work best with equipment that was all made within a year or three of each other. The same year is best, but it doesn't happen all that often. Since we're scrounging rigs, none of our little numbers are going to start with the first two digits that correspond to the year we're presently in. Numbers about five years back seem to be your best bet. Much earlier than that and the equipment either won't work with the rest of your rig, or it's getting obsolete to the point of uselessness even if it does. Sometimes people give things away with stunningly recent numbers. Musta been upgraded by their uncle and they're too stupid to know what they're giving away. Keep this information under your hat. (Now you may ask, "Won't such dishonesty lead to bad karma?" The answer is no! Giving away free computers involves a lot of hard work and time. Little bonuses like this are exactly why you're throughputting all the junk, paraphernalia, components, and whatnot. But if you're the least little bit squeamish about keeping something like this, then by all means tell the nice people what you found in their garbage and see if they want it back. I've done this a time or three myself over the years and have yet to hand anything back to anybody!)

Business end of a video card.

Video Cards

Another joy to play around with is video cards. Hope that your machine has video already built into the motherboard; otherwise, you're gonna discover that lots of video cards will act funny (or not act at all) with a lot of computers.

On rare occasions, video card tweakery can have unexpected disastrous results in places that you'd never think to look, like your BIOS! (This is the basic input/output system. We'll talk more about it later.)

Don't laugh, I've had it happen.

Change a video card and suddenly all your BIOS settings have been wiped clean and the computer will stop dead in its tracks, advising you that there is no boot device or some such similar evilness.

For that matter, more than just video cards can do this. If the machine was doing fair to partly fine while you were first messing around with it and all of a sudden it goes haywire, check your BIOS. I just had that happen with a memory upgrade.

Stuff like that isn't SUPPOSED to happen, but when you're dealing with cast-off machines, expect the unexpected, OK?

Gamers are a great source of video cards. These idiots are always attempting to get the latest, greatest, mostest, bestest, coolest video display available on the planet at any given hour, so they toss their old video cards. These are people with computers that have motherboards that come fully equipped with built-in video display adapters and then go out and drop a pair of C-notes on a video card. I *did* say these people are idiots, didn't I?

Otherwise, all you really need to know about a video card is: does it work? Drop it in the slot and fire that puppy up to *see*. But don't be so quick to throw away cards that don't work. I've seen more than my share of "dead" video cards that all of a sudden sprang to vigorous life when placed in that certain machine they were always waiting for. Generally speaking, your video adapter specs are the first thing to flicker across your machine's screen as it wakes up and comes to life. Unless, of course, you're running some kind of screwed-up eMachine or Dell or something that splashes a corporate logo at you while the machine goes through its POST (power-on self test) routines. (They're advertising their product to people who have *already bought it*. How stupid is that?) Sometimes you can hit the "pause" button if it goes by too fast to read. It'll tell you how many megabytes of memory your video adapter is running. The more megabytes, the better. When giving machines away, always use working video cards that use the least megabytes of memory. Keep the good stuff for yourself, since you're doing this for free.

And oh yeah, one other thing. Go have a look at the socket on the back of your video adapter right now. Take the wire to the monitor out, so you can see it. Now count the rows of holes in it. There's three of 'em, right? At least I hope so. If there's only two rows of holes, you need to throw your video card away and go scrounge one with three rows of holes. And while you're at it, you're gonna need to get a new monitor. Two rows of holes (or pins for the monitor plug) means either horrendous partial-color display (splashes of bright, primary colors, zero color shading, hue, or tone) or no color at all. College students don't really need full color to grind out term papers and shoot 'em to the printer, but everybody else does. Especially folks who would like to play around on the Internet. If you're giving away a machine with crippled graphics capabilities, be sure to advise the recipient of that ahead of time, OK? Yes indeed, people *do* actually get pissed off and gripe at you over things their free computer fails to do to their satisfaction. Go figure.

Sound Cards

Sound cards are similar to video cards. More or less the exact same deal, although I have yet to see a sound card wipe my BIOS. But now that I just wrote that, I'll probably get three in a row that do exactly that. Oh well.

One thing that sound cards do more than video cards is require squirrelly device drivers to make them go. When your machine fails to get your sound card going (or even simply fails to discover that it's there), you're gonna need to go on the Internet and track down the driver files that run your card. Just yesterday (04-29-03, one week to the day fol-

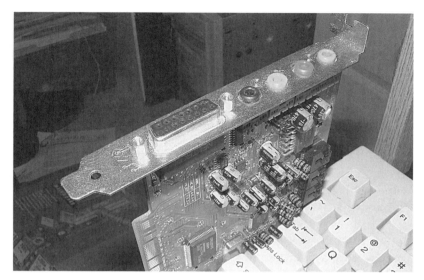

Business end of a sound card.

lowing a dreamlike surf session at Monster Hole, complete
with sparkly, warm, clear, blue-green water, flawless bowl-
ing peaks coming in well overhead, and a more or less clue-
less crowd that couldn't seem to find the lineup, thus giving
me *every last one* of those juicy wave-of-the-set rights that
were spinning into the channel) I cobbled a machine
together that Windoze would NOT recognize the sound card
in, forcing me to install driver files for an ancient
SoundBlaster card that subsequently forced me to *register*
the damn thing (only way to make the damnable registration screen go away on every boot). I'm guessing that the
guys in SoundBlaster Central, where such rubbish gets
dumped, have by now given the folks who cooked up *that*
little plan the stern lecture that they have so truly earned.
Registration crud oughtta have an expiration date, beyond
which nobody cares anyway.

I've never been too big on sound cards in computers
anyway. I'm just as happy as a clam if it won't say a peep.
If I wanted my computer to act like a television, I'd have

Sticks-o-memory.

gotten a television. But since I gave away my last TV back in 1998, I'm not really too dialed in on that sort of thing.

Memory Chips

More weirdness. Memory chips are just as quirky as can be. When they start to go bad, they're capable of doing all sorts of goofy stuff to your machine, including acting badly in one machine while acting el perfecto in another machine. Memory chips come in two basic flavors: small and large. In a rare departure from most things having to do with computers, the large ones actually hold more memory than the small ones. But the small ones seem better behaved. Which is not to say that they behave well, just somewhat better than their ill-tempered brethren.

Memory comes in a bewildering array of subtypes. Speed, capacity, physical specs, phase of moon—hell, there's no end to it.

Drop it in the slot and see if it works. Memory is one of those things that displays across your screen as your machine is first starting up. Since memory routinely lies, don't be so sure that your 32 MB of small memory is really a set of four 8-MB memory chips. It might be a set of four 32-MB chips that's reporting a bogus result to your machine. And if it is, you're actually in possession of 128 MB of memory, something that will make WinXP dance and sing.

If your memory does work, then the only other thing you need to know is that more is always better. Period. At least for your own machine. Giveaway rigs are another matter. Win9x will work reasonably well with 8 MB of memory and up as long as you don't go asking it to do too much at any given time. Everybody seems to think that WinXP needs 128 MB, but 64 will do just fine once you've gone into your "services" menu and disabled all that memory-gobbling crap that otherwise defaults to "automatic."

But be aware that not only does the stuff lie, it also occasionally sabotages your machine. I've seen no end of machines that went into a black funk upon being tested with memory they didn't like. Sometimes the machine will simply quit altogether and you'll have to unplug it and let it sit overnight before it will come out of its sulk and boot back up. Why this is, I have no earthly idea. But it sure the hell *is*, I can tell you that. Hit the power button and all you get is the power-supply fan and the CPU fan. Sometimes not even that. No disk drives, no monitor, no nuthin! Walk away from it when it starts this sort of thing. There's nothing you can do, and all that can happen from this point on is you becoming sufficiently pissed off to throw the whole sorry mess out by the curb for the trash guys to come and haul off. Don't be so hasty, OK?

Sometimes the machine will freeze in mid-boot due to memory weirdness. And then, on the third or fourth boot attempt, all of a sudden it springs to life and everything works just fine and dandy. Why? Dunno. As long as the machine is showing some signs of life at bootup, keep booting for a while. You may get lucky.

Memory routinely bollixes your BIOS for some daffy reason. Always spot-check your BIOS if you encounter strange goings-on when playing around with memory.

Memory weirdness can also cause other things to fail. When a new CD drive that you know to be fully functional inexplicably won't work, suspect your memory among other potential perpetrators. Why? Dunno.

In machines with those damnable power supplies that don't have an honest on/off power switch (but instead have some little dinky thing that attaches to the motherboard via a pair of laughably thin wires), things can get nasty. I just toasted a 128-MB memory chip in one of those rigs, which all of a sudden switched itself *on* when I started working the memory chip into its slot! Smell of burnt electronics. Dead memory chip. Dead computer too. Damn thing STILL isn't booting up. May have toasted the whole works!

When working with those things, be sure to remove the power cord from the back of the machine before you go dropping things into open slots!

The good news about memory is that small memory is now more or less obsolete—32-MB sticks of that stuff aren't worth *anything* anymore; they're just lying around like shells on the beach. For machines that still possess slots that will accept them, four of these puppies will do a nice job. Cool, huh?

Mices

Messed-up mices will completely shut down your computing operation. Better make sure we know what's going on with the furry vermin, eh?

Mice come in three flavors with an occasional weirdie fourth flavor that you'll probably never see. There's serial mices, PS2 mices, USB mices, and bus mices. Actually, with a bus mouse the mouse is just the same, but the socket it plugs into is on the back of a card that you drop into an open slot just like a modem, or sound card, or something like that. Nowadays, that sort of thing is completely useless, but just in case you find a card that's got a mouse (!) socket on the back of it, of all weird-ass things, you'll know what

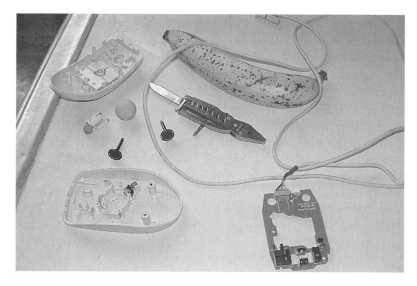

Exploded serial port mouse with banana and full tool kit.

it's for. I've *never* heard of a mouse plug going bad on a computer, but if it ever happens and you just happen to have that wonderful little card that a bus mouse plugs into, you're still in business. Your odds of ever seeing such an alignment of planets are right in there with being hit on the head by a meteorite while walking down the sidewalk. I wouldn't worry about it if I were you.

Of the three "normal" flavors, serial mices are totally obsolete, PS2 mices are rapidly becoming obsolete, and USB mices are becoming the standard.

This is good, because everybody is jumping on the USB bandwagon. Since some of the new machines now come with neither a serial port nor a PS2 port, those types of mices are now showing up as freebies far and wide across this great land of ours because people's new machines have *nowhere* to plug the damn things into. Way cool!

Used to be (and once in a while still is) serial mices would play fits with your modem, and that's one of the main reasons that they have been rendered obsolete. But nowadays modems have gotten somewhat better behaved, and this problem is becoming something of a memory of the bad old days. If you have a serial mouse, use it if you can. Nothing else will ever go into that serial port anyway, right?

If people are giving mices away and you've already got a whole bag of 'em, take the new ones anyway. Mice are mechanical devices and prone to all the slings and arrows that outrageous fortune deals out to such contrivances. Moving parts must eventually fail. Spares are our friends.

With mice it's generally them little wheel-on-a-stick diddy-bops inside of 'em that go bad.

When the little stick gets crudded up with deskgoopy, your cursor arrow starts refusing to scroll nice and smoothly across the page. It'll go *right next* to where you want it, and then steadfastly refuse to move one more damn pixel to allow you to click to download BonziBUDDY. And then when it *does* finally move, it will jump clear across to the other side of the screen in one dizzying leap. When this happens, take your mouse apart (always being careful to

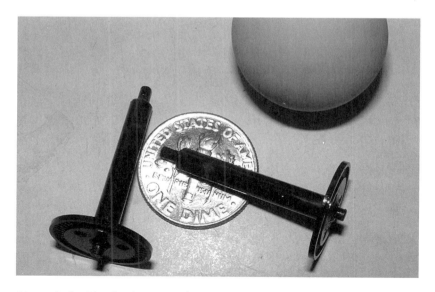

Mouse ball with wheels on a stick.

look for hidden screws that hold the thing together up under some sticker or other) and wipe off the stick doodads with a paper towel or something. Get all that belly-button lint off the sticks and they'll spin nice and easy. But if some dork or other has *scraped* the crud off the sticks on some dark day in the past, you're more or less sunk. Unsmooth sticks are a major magnet for more deskgoopy. Any roughness or nicks on the sticks will invariably have you taking the damn thing apart once again to clean it up, sooner instead of later. Save that mouse to give to somebody you don't like. And while you're at it in there, be sure to give the little ball a cleaning too. Warm soapy water, alcohol, whatever. Just don't use anything that will leave any residue. Residue = deskgoopy.

Once in a while you'll get a mouse that's pristine clean inside and still acts wonky. Maybe it moves fine and dandy vertically but not horizontally, or vice versa.

Open it up and take a gander at where the little wheels go. Somewhere down there, there's a notch in the circuit board that allows the wheel to fit into it (take note of those little perforations around the perimeter of the wheel) and on either side of the notch there's gonna be a little doodad attached to the circuit board on a very short wire or two. One of these little gizmos shoots a beam of invisible light at the other one and the beam of light shines through those perforations on the perimeter of the wheel. Each perforation going by as the wheel is spun by that little ball counts as another click as the cursor is moved pixel by pixel across your screen. Yep, that little Rube Goldberg methodology is exactly what makes your mouse go. Anyhoo, if the two gizmos aren't looking at each other squarely enough, then your mouse is gonna become defective as the detector gizmo fails to acknowledge some or all of the little invisible beams of light that are supposed to be shining through the perforations in the wheel.

Bend these two things around some and then put your

Photoelectric sensors. For some weird reason, this mouse has TWO (!) on each wheel.

mouse back together and see if that helped. If not, do it some more. Don't be afraid of breaking something: The mouse is already broken—can't do it any further harm. Often as not, this will magically tune the mouse right up into a state of perfect functionality. (Thank me for this little trick by telling your brother-in-law to buy a copy of this book, OK?)

And no, I do not know how the little lights can get out of alignment in the first place. Kinda makes you wonder what people are doing with their mouses when nobody's looking.

As for laser mices, they're still too expensive and nobody's giving 'em away yet. And since nobody's ever given one to me, I've never had the opportunity to take it apart and play around with it. I'm quite sure that they've got their own dippy little world of peculiarities, but so far

I'm ignorant of the whole place.

Keyboards

Keyboards are humdrum devices, but without a functioning one your computer becomes just an annoying box of junk. Considering the whackings that they take, the miracle is that keyboards work *at all*.

No keyboard present, press F1 to continue.

While it's true that you can load an OS and otherwise sort of get along (in a crippled kind of way) without a mouse, nothing of the kind will work without a functioning keyboard.

Lucky for us, keyboards more or less grow on trees; if a keyboard breaks, it's more or less a trivial assignment to come up with another one. Dead computers almost always show up with fully functioning keyboards. This leads to a nice stash of spare keyboards lying around should you ever need one.

Keyboards come in two flavors: ones with fat connector plugs and ones with thin connector plugs. The fat ones are completely obsolete nowadays, which means that if you're in possession of an older cast-off computer, you're gonna *need* one of these puppies. So whenever they come by, grab 'em! They're not making 'em anymore. (Why did they decide to change this? I see *nothing* that was gained.)

Thin-connector-plug keyboards are stupid. And the reason they're stupid is that the plug they use is exactly the same plug that your PS2 mouse uses. Whose idea was *that*? Dumb. And the two identical plugs are always located right next to each other on the back of your machine. Dumber.

Sometimes the plugs on the mouse and keyboard are color-coded so that total idiots can match the purple on the plug to the purple ring around the socket on the back of the machine and make sure they haven't plugged their mouse-'n'-keyboard in backward. I suppose this was a laudable idea when it was cooked up, but nowadays you can easily find yourself (using cast-off parts cobbled together from here, there, and everywhere) plugging the purple plug on the mouse into the purple-ringed socket for your keyboard by mistake. Dumbest. Pay attention back there when plugging this stuff in, OK?

And by the way, sometimes when you plug the mouse-'n'-keyboard in backward, the damn thing will still work! Or at least work just enough to fake you out and then exhibit bizarre behavior later on that you may, or may not, know means you need to go back and check it just to make sure it's OK. You have been warned.

Sometime when not much is going on, take a keyboard apart just for giggles and marvel at the amazing amount of lint, fuzz, grass clippings, and mastodon bones that have accumulated up under where the keys go. Things that get spilled onto keyboards disappear just far enough for you to not be able to see them when the keyboard is still in one piece. But every last bit of it is still in there somewhere. Makes the miracle that keyboards even work that much more miraculous.

Occasionally, wonky keyboards can be taken into the shower with you and given a good bath with salutary effects. Don't even need to take 'em apart lots of times. Just rinse the living hell out of 'em and then set 'em somewhere to dry out nice and good for a couple of days. I've found that when setting them down to dry, placing them on edge seems to work better because the water (and all that filth that has emulsified into the water) will run downhill some-where to the very edge of something. Your mileage may vary. If you're not sure, you can pluck all the keys off the keyboard before doing this. Just make sure you memorize (or better, make a map or take a picture) the location of every last key so that you can reassemble things to their correct configuration. Keys just sort of snap into and out of place with no actual fastener or anything. Tweezers, needle-nose pliers, or something like that oughtta work. Don't go prying them from one side with a table knife or screwdriver though—you'll likely as not generate sufficient rotational movement to snap the little plastic thing and then you're *done for,* with zero option for fixing the damage you just caused. Be careful.

Floppy-Disk Drives

Not too much I can add to what I've already said about floppy-disk drives, except for maybe "Keep the peanut butter out of 'em." Soon enough the things will be no more than a fading memory, as the Mac people have been earnestly attempting to cause to happen for years now. Finally looks like everybody else is climbing onboard, which is unfortunate, owing to the fact that for storing and transporting (in your shirt pocket and other supereasy kinds of places) things like text files, nothing beats a floppy and probably never will. I heartily believe in Keeping It Simple, Stupid, and using a 700-MB storage disk to take a 3-kilobyte file to a machine that isn't hooked to any network strikes me as similar to using a barbell to swat at houseflies on a hot summer afternoon. (Machines such as this will always exist, so don't even *think* about giving me any crap about the coming ubiquity of the 'Net.) Floppy boot disks are also spectacularly useful at times.

I *did* mention about the chances for hooking your data cable upside down and I need to reiterate that right here, right now. I *know* this stuff and it still happens to me anyway. Never put the case back on a rig till you've tested the whole thing, floppies in particular. Otherwise you'll always end up removing the case to fix this or that little stupidity that you forgot to button up correctly.

Check your BIOS if the floppy don't work too. "NONE"

popping up in the BIOS where your "A" drive oughtta be is just too common to believe.

CD Drives

Well now, we're just getting into the zone where every computer you might get for free is finally arriving with its own CD drive, and now they're talking about phasing them out because they're obsolete. Gotta love progress, eh?

My guess is that the things are gonna be around for more than just a little while yet.

One of the main reasons you'll get a loose CD drive for free is misplaced jumpers. I just last month received a nice 48x Lite-On drive in perfect working order from an office that had placed it in their scrap heap. The jumper was set to "cable select." When I plugged it into any of my test rigs and moved the jumper to either one of the other settings (master/slave) it worked just fine and dandy and the POST routine picked it up immediately. Tra la la. Does anybody even *use* "cable select" anymore? My guess is "no," but it's nice of it to be there as an option to cause me to get even more free stuff

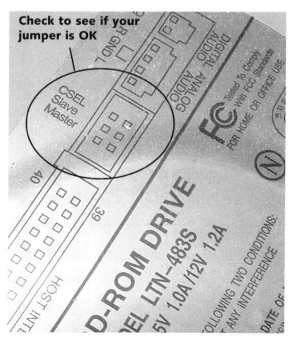

Read these stickers on your hardware and then go check to see if the jumper is set correctly.

that works like a champ once it's been configured correctly.

This is the sort of happenstance that REALLY makes me wonder what is going on with the professional guys who work on systems for businesses. If a computer goes "boink" and quits working, are these people really SO stupid that they don't know to check the jumpers on the back of the parts they remove from the dead machines? I can understand giving the entire machine away. Replacing the whole machine is oftentimes cheaper than spending 100 bucks an hour for some white-shirted guy to pluck pieces and parts out of it, test 'em, and then find another machine to plug 'em in to. But to actually remove the CD drive and then not know enough to check the jumpers? Man, that's just weird!

Aside from checking the jumpers, there's not a whole lot you can do with a CD drive that's in a poor frame of mind except maybe for verifying that the ribbon cable is on the pins right side up and isn't offset to one side or another. This can happen when somebody cracks the little plastic thing that holds the cable (or perhaps it doesn't even *have* a little plastic thing that holds the cable).

Generally speaking, when they're dead, they're dead. Once in a while a CD will refuse to work in anything except some certain machine. I have no idea why this is, but it is. So if you've got a dead one, be sure to periodically plug it in to new machines as they come through your door. Every so often, all of a sudden it lights right up—bingo! After a while, though, this trial and error becomes tiresome, at which point you may toss the whole contraption out since it's taking up room and time and isn't doing anybody a whole lot of good.

CDs work by using a little laser beam to read the disk. Lasers are optical devices and must involve the use of a lens somewhere along the line. Lenses, being made of clear glass, don't like to get crudded up with dust or dead cockroach wings. If you've got a CD that's acting wonky even though the POST picks it right up and your BIOS is set to "auto" and well aware of its existence, you might benefit from taking it apart and going after the lens. Clean the lens with alcohol and some wipe paper that doesn't leave a cloud of lint particles on the glass in its wake. Holding the lens with a pair of tweezers or something while you're rubbing away at it with a piece of toilet paper globbed onto the end of a toothpick is in direct violation of my imprecation to avoid the lint-generating kind of wipe paper. Check the innards for cockroach wings that might have become lodged between the lens and where the disk goes. Remove all the belly-button lint while you're in there too.

Just be advised that getting to this area is oftentimes *incredibly pesty and annoying.* The folks who make CD drives don't really want you in there poking around with their stuff, and they design it accordingly. So what winds up happening a lot of times is that you spend a whole afternoon messing around with the thing, only to discover that your double extra perfect mission to clean the lens didn't do a damn bit of good and the thing *still* doesn't work right.

All of the above applies with equal force and effect for DVDs and anything else that spins a platter while shooting at it with a small laser.

Hard Drives

Oh boy! Now we get to play with some really cool stuff! Hard drives just ROCK!

What could be cooler than a little square metal dingus with a nice heft to it, with neat-o circuitry exposed on one side like a superminiature cityscape set from a *Star Wars* movie, with a little green light on it sometimes that tells you it's doing something, and innards right out of some science fiction movie that include mirrored disks that spin like crazy while a little arm gizmo flickers back and forth across them like a snake's tongue?

Yeah buddy, hard drives are COOL!

And you can put the whole world in 'em too! Phenomenal amounts of information go on those spinning disks like a skyscraper-size genie goes into a bottle. Movies,

Hard drives.

music, letters, pictures, games, finances, battle plans—hell, there's no end to it!

Get a useless hard drive (anything less than a gig or three is now considered useless, although I fondly remember a time when I thought that 40 MB was just *enormous*) and see if you can take the cover off without causing it to become catatonic. Then fire it up and watch and listen as it does its thing! (You might need a little Torx screwdriver to do this. Since you will *never* repair a hard drive by opening it up, I refuse to include this little specialty item as a part of your tool kit.)

Total coolness! But be careful, OK? If one of them disks comes loose while it's hammering around at a zillion rpms, it can send shrapnel into your eye faster than you can say "blind guy." You have been WARNED!

OK, enough of that crap. What the hell can we do with a hard drive while the cover's *on*?

Not a whole lot, actually.

Mechanically, your options are even fewer than what you have with a CD. All you get to play with is the cable and the jumpers. That's it! Unfortunately, for some daffy reason, the jumpers on hard drives are weird. And sometimes, you'll discover that certain hard drives will not work in the presence of other hard drives but will act just as sweet as a little lamb when solo or in the company of somebody else's hard drive. You just putz around with 'em to find this kind of stuff out. Trial and error. Plan on a lot of error.

Jumpers on hard drives are complete showstoppers when set incorrectly. When Joe Wannabee decides to "fix" his girlfriend's computer and then further decides to move the jumpers around on the backs of the hard drives and then further forgets where the jumpers were originally (you'll soon discover that this kind of foolishness happens ALL the time), you wind up with a free computer and Joe has to go find a new girlfriend.

Lots of hard drives come with little diagrams of how the jumpers should go. This usually shows up on the case or perhaps on a little sticker that's glued to the case. I've also seen 'em fresh from the factory, with this bit of priceless information covered up with an additional sticker. These

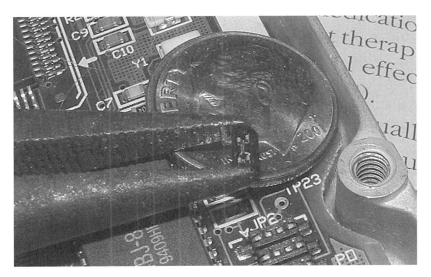

Sometimes jumpers on hard drives are too small to believe!

additional stickers never have anything useful on them, unless you think that "234nj8934 = 9 Taiwan" or perhaps "warranty void if removed" might be useful.

Fortunately, if the jumper settings peeled off with the damnable extra sticker, you can just go to the Internet and Google up the specs for your hard drive. Amongst the specs will be your jumper settings. Pay CLOSE attention to your hard drive's jumper settings. I cannot begin to tell you how many times that jumpers have been the cause of a system that wasn't working right, and this includes systems that *I* had assembled.

Once in a while you'll encounter a hard drive that will not work when jumpered as a "master" but will work just fine and dandy when jumpered as a "slave." Or the reverse. Either way, don't sweat it. Just use the drive the way it works and don't worry about it. You'll always need drives configured both ways. More on that in a bit.

Another thing about hard drives is the way they have been configured by the software to operate. Brand "A" software *hates* brand "B" software, or perhaps brand "MS" software, and will calmly inform you that your hard drive either doesn't exist, has no data on it, is about a tenth of its real size, or any number of other completely bogus pieces of misinformation. Since this isn't a physical problem (well, actually it is, but I'm not including the temporary arrangement of magnetic zones on your hard drive's platters as properly physical) but a software problem, I'll deal with it in the software department of this book.

That being the case, it sure the hell *looks* like a physical problem anyway. Do not be fooled when your computer refuses to work and displays cheerful information like "no fixed disk present" or things equally sinister when starting up. To quote an old FidoNet tagline: "Who's General Failure, and why's he reading my hard disk?"

Another quite weird problem with hard drives is "stiction." (Like "suction" but with the word "stick" instead of the word "suck.") Hard drives, when left powered off long enough, will sometimes stick and refuse to spin up when powered on. No spinning platter, no functioning hard drive. You can listen for this problem and feel it too. It's a sound you won't hear and a feeling you won't feel.

Spinning platters in your hard drive generally make a very soft whirring sound. Listen for it when you first power on your computer. It's not that grindy/grumbly sound that the read/write heads make. If you hold a powered-on drive in your hand, you immediately become aware of its very peculiar gyroscopic feel. It won't want to turn in certain directions and will actually apply a noticeable force to your hand when you rotate it in the proper direction.

A drive with stiction does neither of these things. The platters aren't spinning: no whirr, no gyroscope.

At first, try repeated power-on/power-off cyclings of your stuck hard drive. Sometimes that's all it takes.

If this doesn't work, more drastic measures are called for. Tap the side of the case with a screwdriver blade. Give it a nice sharp whap, but not too sharp. If this doesn't do the trick, try it again while the drive is powered on. I've literally had them come to life right in the palm of my hand following this trick.

Sometimes when this fails to work, merely setting the drive aside for a few days after the whapping seems to be what the doctor ordered. Power it on next week and—hey, presto!—it's happy as a clam.

Drives that have been brought to life following an attack of stiction are *not to be trusted*. They will fail again, sometimes alarmingly soon. Put 'em in machines as backup drives only. Put 'em in machines you're giving to people you aren't overly fond of. They may outlive your dog, but don't count on it.

And while we're at it here, don't go whapping on drives that are already working. The read/write head is flicking back and forth about the thickness of a standard-size molecule of beer away from the surface of that insanely whirling platter. "Head strikes" aren't very groovy at all and will result from any jiggling, juggling, or jangling of a spinning hard drive. Don't do it.

Why You MUST Have a Pair of
Hard Drives in Your Machine

Since hard drives are the whole reason for having a computer, anything that affects your hard drive will affect your entire computing experience. (Besides storing data, what real good *is* a computer anyway?) Anything that's on your hard drive is gone if your hard drive craps out, and it's gone anyway if you're one of those unfortunate fools who likes to do numb-nutted things like press "Y" after being prompted with "Warning! Formatting your hard drive will erase ALL data! Proceed? Press 'Y' for yes."

Sad fact of the matter is that everything can affect your hard drive, and it's always adversely! From beer spills, to lightning strikes, to house fires, to floods, to malicious children, to you name it. Some of this stuff will get you, your house, and everything in it. For that kind of thing, there's not a whole lot you can do. Less catastrophic deals, on the other hand, can be kept more or less manageable by backing up *every bit of* your personal data on a backup hard drive.

As it turns out, most of what's considered crucial data falls under the heading of text files, be they spreadsheets, word processor documents, secret codes, or whatever. And text files are the smallest things you will be dealing with. This is nice because it allows you to throw one of those uselessly small hard drives, which you will invariably accumulate as you do this sort of thing, into your box as an IDE primary slave, secondary master, or secondary slave. Motherboards come with a pair of IDE connectors already installed, one primary and one secondary. They'll be the only things on your motherboard that a ribbon cable from a hard drive will fit onto. Make sure the ribbon cable is on frontward (mind Pin 1, please) and your hard drives are jumpered properly. If you've got SCSI, well then you can string this stuff together endlessly. Why stop at FOUR major doodads? Anyway, use the spare drive(s) inside your machine to send backups of all your personal data to. Leave the OS, your porn, and your stolen Madonna soundtracks on your primary master and don't worry about it. That stuff can be reinstalled from disk or downloaded from www.you'reanidiot.com again whenever you want to. Personal data, once gone, stays that way forever.

Check your backup drive periodically to make sure it's happy and working as it should. If it gets a little wonky, double-check that everything you need really is on your primary drive and then throw the backup away and replace it with another backup and then reload all that stuff from your primary on to your new backup. Tedious? Yes. Lifesaving? Eventually.

I've found that deliberately putting a program or two that I use on a regular basis on to my backup drive will force me to run that drive fairly often, thus checking the integrity of that drive fairly often.

And while you're at it here, copy that stuff to CD too.

Why You MUST Have Two Machines, Now That I Think of It

Indeed, one machine, when broken, is just about as useful as one hard drive, also when broken.

You're accumulating rigs, so go ahead and get one of the crappier ones, or even one of the good ones, and set up a secondary system. Tertiary is becoming a bit excessive, and quaternary has entered the land of obsessive behavior. Having said that, I must admit to possessing *more* than this many working rigs at any one time over the years, perhaps even right this minute. Hell, I just like computers! So sue me!

Your backup computer need not have its own monitor, mouse, keyboard, or whatever. Just the box is all you really need. Switch the wires around from your primary machine whenever you want to use the backup. The more peripherals the better, but don't let the lack of a keyboard or monitor cause you to give up and quit.

A secondary machine will bail your sorry self out of the hole it's in when your primary machine farts sideways for no good reason and you need to get online to receive and reply to a career-changing e-mail *tonight*! This kind of thing happens far more often than you'd like to believe. Once you get in with this computer jazz, you'll discover it's kind of like getting in with the mafia. Once you're in, you're in. May as well have yourself together, eh?

Down here in Florida, summertime is lightning time. People and equipment are fried on a regular basis. Talk to anybody in Florida and I'll guarantee you that if they're computer savvy and have been that way for more than a year or two, they'll have a story or two to tell you about friends, family, acquaintances, or themselves that involves Thor's thunderbolts raining down from above and hitting something squarely! Goodbye, sweet computer!

It's bad enough around here that I've finally had to come to terms with the fact that even if I unplug the damn things (which I do religiously on days when the cumulonimbus boils far into the stratosphere), a bolt of lightning might just decide to come through the window and hit them *directly*. There's nothing any of us can do about it, except maybe move to Barrow, Alaska, or somewhere else where they don't have lightning. For myself, I ain't moving.

Many other things are also fully capable of finishing off your computer. Plan ahead and have a working substitute when that dark day arrives, OK?

The Stuff You Find on Hard Drives

I'm not here to tell you how to hack Social Security numbers off a used hard drive. Is that clear? What I do want to do is clue you into the fact that a truly amazing amount of critical information—personal, corporate, even military—can be plucked off the hard drives on cast-off computers. I mentioned earlier that using anything that's not really yours will invariably result in a karma payback that you will not like, and by golly I just mentioned it again!

People just *will not* clean hard drives the way they're supposed to when upgrading equipment and getting rid of the old machines. I dunno. Human nature, I guess. The Slacker Gene.

Stuff will show up plainly labeled, or it will be buried on a formatted drive. It may be loud and clear or it may be soft and blurry or it may be a combination of the two. Lots of time weirdie partitions that come up doggo on OS "A" will tell all when approached with OS "B." Yet another reason to learn every kind and flavor of OS that you can. Which, now that I think of it, just might be why you'd be stumbling around six separate working rigs in your room, each running a different OS or variant thereof.

Hard drives that "die" will come back to life after being left on the shelf for a couple of years and then blab every last secret that they contain to a total stranger who wasn't even looking for secrets.

Hard drives that have been formatted will yield up their data to those who know the game well. Loose platters, plucked from a dead hard drive, can be caused to reveal many things.

What I'm really trying to do here is keep you from stepping into this sort of hole yourself. Be very careful about what you put on your computer's hard drive. There are persons and organizations out there with some serious horsepower when it comes to extracting information off computers. If there's something on your machine that you'd like nobody to ever find out about, I suggest melting the hard drive down. Otherwise, you can never be sure somebody won't find it.

CMOS Battery

This little guy is sufficiently weird that I couldn't just roll it into the general motherboard section.

It's a little silver coin-looking thing most of the time, although on certain ancient rigs it will be a small barrel wired to the motherboard, maybe an inch long, maybe less.

If it's the barrel, you're screwed, two ways in fact. The obvious way is that any battery will eventually rot and leak nasty battery stuff on whatever it's lying on/in. Your little barrel will do this too. And since it's sitting on your motherboard, that's not good. Nasty corrosive battery spooge and printed circuit boards do not mix. The unobvious way is that if you've got a motherboard with the

CMOS battery.

little barrel battery, you're dealing with something from the Silurian, before even *dinosaurs* were invented. Give it to your brother-in-law. The one you don't like.

If it's the little coin, things are much better. In the first place, you can replace it when it goes bad. And bad CMOS batteries will cause your machine to act unpleasantly. Even though it's called a "CMOS" battery, the thing that goes down the flusher when it craps out is your BIOS. Suddenly your machine doesn't have the faintest idea what a hard drive is. "Please insert boot media and press Enter." Yeah, right. Get into your BIOS setup and fix things after you replace the battery. Most of the time they last forever, so you will accumulate them as you process machines. Mind the voltages on your replacement batteries though. Don't wanna cause any trouble *that* way.

Cache

Cache is from somewhere between the Silurian and the dinosaurs, back when any expedient to try to make your machine run a little quicker was a good thing. It's a little memory stick-looking deal, sitting up on its edge all by itself, somewhere on your motherboard's back 40. Won't fit in any memory slot, and memory won't fit in your cache slot. The stuff is gone bye-bye nowadays, subsumed into the generalized circuitry of your machine.

I've got a couple of sticks of cache lying around, but they're more trouble than they're worth. They're just like memory in that they come in too many flavors and each is incompatible with all the rest. They'll lock up your machine if they aren't the right kind, and even when they're properly matched, you still can't really tell that they're actually DOING anything.

If you have a machine with cache and it works, leave it alone. If you have a machine with no cache and it works, leave it alone. If you've got a full day to play around with, and it's raining or snowing outside and you don't wanna bother with that, then putz around with your cache. Who knows, you just may wreck your entire machine.

Cool, huh?

MONITORS

Without one of these babies, your computer becomes just a box-o-wires, unable to communicate with you except for perhaps some plaintive beeps on start-up and a blinken-light or two. Whaddaya say we take a look at it then?

Once upon a time, monitors were a major chokepoint on the road to free machines. The damn things cost money and people would *not* let go of them. New machine, old monitor. Net result: You get the old machine and they keep the damn monitor.

But no more. Hallelujah! The liberation of the monitors has begun and is rapidly approaching the point of full steam ahead.

Express your sincere thanks and appreciation for this by saying something nice about flat-panel displays. Solid state. No cathode-ray tube. No heavy, awkward box. No fragile dingus that might explode if you drop it. You, of course, will still have to put up with that kind of trouble 'cause people aren't giving away their flat-panel monitors just yet.

Do We Remember about Electrocution?

While it's fine and dandy to be opening up your computer's case and poking around inside there like a mole digging for roots, the same cannot be said for your monitor.

You try that with a monitor and they'll be looking for your next of kin to notify in pretty short order.

Monitors have things inside them like "B +" and "flyback transformers." These sorts of

Deadly danger lurks within.

things, and other things too, will attempt to kill you, and since they are capable of producing voltages in the *thousands* of volts, you don't even have to properly touch them to get killed. They'll cheerfully send out a little blue finger of death to wick you directly into tomorrow's obituary section.

Since you're not going to be poking around inside of a monitor that's working properly, any monitor you do enter will, likely as not, be capable of doing something it's not supposed to, perhaps frying your silly ass.

Just stay the hell out of there, OK?

With one exception. Well, maybe two.

And before we go any further here, let me advise you that the people who make monitors really don't want you inside of 'em and make the cases correspondingly difficult to remove. Hidden screws and sneak catches and latches are the norm. They're trying to tell you something. Perhaps you should *listen* to them, eh?

For those of you who don't listen, and are perhaps also endowed with a bit of a death wish, let us proceed.

Sometimes monitors get all blurry and people get rid of them before they go cross-eyed. Certain monitors have little adjustment knobs inside of them for focus; some have a single knob, some have a pair of them. They'll be little plastic guys, usually down near the bottom at the back end of the monitor with a slot in the end of the stick that's facing you. (Stay away from the middle and front end of a monitor when it's running, or you'll die.) This slot is for the insertion of a screwdriver blade so you can twist the little knob without having to put your big, fat, clumsy fingers in there, perhaps bumping the wrong thing and getting killed. Be advised, however, that since your screwdriver blade is nice conductive metal, if you bump the wrong thing with it, you'll probably die anyway. Somewhere right next to the knob will be a little bit of plastic with the word "focus" on it. If that word isn't there, then you're going to be twiddling the wrong knob. *Don't do it.*

Basically, what you're doing in there is working on a live bomb—one that will kill you if you set it off by mistake. (You'd do this on purpose? Never mind.) You're the Bomb Squad guy. Be careful, Indiana, or you'll be dead, dead, dead!

Anyhoo, twist the knob and then look at the picture. If you're lucky, it'll come into nice, crisp focus. If you're unlucky, it will get better, but it won't quite adjust to where you need it and some residual fuzziness will always be there to annoy you. (I've got a nice 17-inch monitor sitting in my pile of spares right this minute that has this problem, although it's hardly noticeable. Thank you, Debbie Knight, for giving me that monitor. I've gotten a world of use out of it.) If you're really unlucky, you'll be dead 'cause you touched the wrong thing.

Something else that monitors do sometimes is flicker weirdly, with shrinking or expanding lines appearing across the screen, or display colors that change erratically, or any number of other goof-ass kinds of things.

If it doesn't say "focus," stay the hell away from it.

If your monitor has electronic adjustment controls, you can forget about what I'm going to say next. For those of you with actual, physical knobs you twist, things are a bit more hopeful. Twistable knobs hook directly to little gizmos that can get crudded up with dust and beer. The little gizmos are called potentiometers, although once in a while you'll encounter some smart-ass who calls 'em "rheostats" just to confuse you.

Oftentimes your potentiometer's case of the cruds translates directly to your picture acting weird as I described above. What you then need to do is clean the crud out of the potentiometer. You may *not* open up the damn thing to do this, however. To do so would break it, leaving you outta luck. Fortunately, there's another way to do it. First off, remove any actual knob to expose the little shaft that comes out of the potentiometer. The "pot" will be just on the other side of the monitor's case. Get your hands on a can of "electrical contact cleaner" and liberally spray the insides of the potentiometer with it. There'll be a hole or two that you can place that thin little straw from the nozzle of your can of contact cleaner into, or at least some clearance around the shaft to allow you to blast away at the area just inside the monitor case. Spray it and twist the knob at the same time. Do it over and over. Stay with it. If the Gods of Nice Display are on your side, you'll discover that you've solved your problem by just spraying it with a can of *stuff*. Elderly housewives who watch TV all day think that this is how everything gets fixed. You just spray some of that *stuff* on it.

This doesn't work all the time. Or even most of the time. But some of the time it does and is therefore worthy of your attentions.

Once in a blue moon, your potentiometers will be on the end of a long plastic stick, necessitating your entry into the innards of your monitor to access them and squirt them with your can of *stuff*. If you have to take the case off the monitor to get to the potentiometers, please go back and read all that noise I just wrote about getting electrocuted in there, OK?

If the above therapies don't do the trick, try giving the damned monitor a nice slap on the side of the case or somewhere to maybe knock a little sense into its head. You never know.

PERIPHERALS

This is stuff that's not really an integral part of your computer, but that you probably have some of anyway. Your computer works just fine without it, but it adds a little something to the overall system. What it is is more damn crap, actually.

I'll probably forget to include something or other that *you* think is simply indispensable (GAMES), but that I've either never heard of (GAMES), never gotten for free

(GAMES), or just loathe and detest sufficiently (GAMES) that I refuse to acknowledge its existence by even mentioning its name (GAMES).

You won't find any game controllers in this section, in case you were wondering.

If you'd like to learn about games and the equipment that runs them, go flag down the first 15-year-old you see with a bone through her nose. I'm sure *she* knows all about games, despite not knowing the capital of the United States of America or perhaps who Adolph Hitler might have been. Game people are like that.

Printers

Really, printers are an integral part of your computer. Without a printer, a computer is hobbled pretty severely in my estimation. Your printer is the business end of your computer when your computer is used as the tool that it was intended to be.

But since they come in a zillion different flavors and live at the end of a long wire, sometimes not even on the same table (or even in the same building sometimes, fer chrissakes!) as your rig, we're just gonna call them the peripherals that they really are.

Free printers abound, but there's almost always something wrong with them, or they're ultraprimitive dot-matrix clonkers.

Dot-matrix printers will work just fine and dandy for those term papers your college-student recipients of free rigs will be churning out and, in a pinch, they'll work for other folks too. Ma and Pa Kettle will be served nicely by a dot-matrix printer when it comes to cranking out those idiotic "one Christmas letter for all 75 members of the family" kinds of deals. (Does anybody remember mimeographed Christmas letters? How weird was *that* stuff?)

I wouldn't suggest putting your résumé together using a dot-matrix printer, but I suppose you could.

About the only real problem with ancient dot-matrix

printers is getting a replacement ribbon for them. This is something I can't help you with. Maybe Google for it. Look on eBay or somewhere. Learn how to re-ink your ribbon or something. I dunno. Other than that, dot-matrix printers seem to have been designed and built to help document the environment following Armageddon and are correspondingly armor-plated and sturdy. Should a problem arise with the mechanical aspects to your dot-matrix (or any other, for that matter) printer, my advice is to simply throw it away and go looking for another printer. Maybe even *buy* one if you need to. Just don't go buying a cheapie, OK? Those low-rent Lexmarks will crap out on you before you can finish printing the first draft of your manuscript. Phoo.

Open up a dead printer if you doubt the wisdom of my words telling you to throw it away. What the hell IS all that stuff in there? Where'd it all come from? What's it DO? Printers are just about as bad as a VCR when it comes to being full of dopey little wheels, belts, doodads, and dinguses. You wanna spend your time learning how to figure that crap out and fix it? Fine for you. As for me, I'm gonna go surfing. See ya.

Newer printers are easier to deal with. Not much to them, really. I've discovered that when people give you a printer, lots of times it's because they've lost the little power supply doodad that plugs into the wall and has a funny-looking little round plug on the end of a thinnish wire that fits into a little hole somewhere down on the side or back of the printer. How they lose these things is beyond me, but lose them they do.

Have a look at your latest acquisition and FIND THAT HOLE. Somewhere right next to it will be a little symbol with information that tells you the DC volts and polarity required to make your printer go. Copy that info down on paper and then do one of two things:

1. Rummage through your 50-lb. pile of them little power-supply doodads that plug into walls and all have a little

round plug on the end of a thinnish wire until you find one that matches your printer. The info will be on the little square thing with the prongs on it that plugs into the wall socket. Voltage *and* polarity (positive outside/negative inside, or the reverse) MUST match. But it really doesn't matter. You'll never find the right little doodad. They come in too many flavors, all of them the *wrong* flavor. This leads directly to option number . . .

2. Go down to your local electronic supply place and just buy the damned thing and be done with it. (Try your best to patronize those weird little mom-and-pop joints as opposed to the big franchise places; you'll get better service and lots of neat-o help that the droids behind the counter at Radio Smack won't know the first thing about.) If you're giving the rig away, maybe keep the receipt and insist that whoever gets the "free" computer reimburse you in cold beer or something for the money you spend on this kind of crap.

Be advised that occasionally you'll get a printer without the power-supply doodad and go out and buy a new one only to discover that the printer is messed up for other reasons and you've just thrown away a sawbuck for nothing. Return the doodad to the store where you bought it and hope they'll give you the sawbuck back. Or just keep it and hope that you'll be able to use it on something else some fine day.

If the printer comes complete with power but doesn't work for other reasons, your hopes dim accordingly.

If your OS is newer than the printer you're dealing with, it should have the device drivers for that brand of printer already buried deep within some damned .cab file or other somewhere. Hook up the printer to your computer (actually, it's better to use one of your secondary rigs for this and leave your primary rig the hell and gone alone), turn the printer on, and go through the "add printer" rigamaroo by clicking your start button. It's almost always in there with your control panel under the "settings" part of that menu you get when you click start.

Walk through this stuff and hope your OS recognizes the printer. If not, go to the option in the rigamaroo where you can "pick from list" a printer that seems sufficiently similar to what's sitting on the floor next to the test rig. Try it that way. Lots of times this works. Open up Word, or Notepad, or whatever, and press both hands down on the keyboard to generate a "document" and then send that puppy to the printer. It'll either work or it won't work. I don't need to tell a smart guy like you to put paper in the printer first, do I? I didn't think so.

If it works, write down whatever printer you "picked from list" so you can repeat this procedure with the rig you're gonna be giving away some day and then write that information down and tape it to the printer. If you fail to write it down and tape it to the printer, you'll invariably be unable to remember what the hell you did when you finally go back, get the printer from your pile of printers, and hook it up to a machine to give away.

If it doesn't work, repeat the process using different printers you've picked from that list. At first, stay within the same brand. If you've got an HP sitting on the floor hooked up to your test rig, don't go picking anything from Sanyo until you've exhausted every last entry from the HP list. At some point the thing will either start working or you'll get sick and disgusted with all this tedious crap and give up.

If you're lucky, the printer came with its own installation CD. If it did, you can forget everything I just said unless the machine you're working on doesn't have a CD and you are unable for some reason or other to hook a CD drive to it for installing things like printer drivers.

If you've got the CD, be sure to burn a copy of it (check it to make sure it works) to give to the recipient of the machine when you give it away. Keep the original. You'll be glad you did.

Printers that don't work even though they're all device-drivered-up are not a whole lot of fun unless it's just the ink cartridge that's run dry. Yes, that happens too. I've accepted a few perfectly good printers with empty ink cartridges. Not sure what people are thinking when they give 'em away, but that's not my concern.

You'll quickly discover that ink cartridges are NOT a trivial purchase. Frickin' things cost money. It's a total racket, conceived and executed by the corporations that manufacture the printers, designed and implemented to squeeze as much money from the customers as possible.

Lately it's gotten to the point where the manufacturers have embedded expiration software into the cartridges! Yes indeed, old cartridges will crap out merely because the thing is too old! The printer mafia wants you to buy more cartridges and since they haven't figured out a way to send Big Murray the Enforcer to your home to help *persuade* you (yet), this is one of their little methods to get some more of your money. Don't even think about telling me that the ink is gonna spoil like it's a gallon of milk sitting outside on a July afternoon or something.

Circumvent this by resetting the time and date on your test rig (and perhaps your primary rig too, if required) to a time in the past near to when the cartridge was manufactured. Play around with this. Go too far back in the past and that won't work either. Be double extra careful to reset the time and date to the real world when you're done printing, or all sorts of weird stuff will start happening to your e-mail and Bob knows what else.

No telling when the manufacturers will begin to embed something into the cartridges that operates independently and can't be cheated this way. At that point I say we rise up in an angry mob, carrying torches and pitchforks, and march on over to their haunted castle on the hill and burn it to the ground.

After all the above, about the only other thing you can do with a printer is to check the cable. If it lights up, the computer is talking with it in a friendly tone of voice, and the cartridge is OK, then there's really nothing else you can do. I mentioned the cable thing way back in the beginning of this book. Go back and read it again if you have to. Yes indeed, boys and girls, cables do go bad. Have a spare or two known good cables to swap into the test article to make sure that the problem isn't hiding in the wire. (Put 'em on your own machine and print something just to make sure.) Wiggle the connections. Whatever.

Speakers

Not much you can do with speakers. They more or less either work or they don't. Sometimes they require one of them power supply doodads that plug into the wall, the same way that printers (and a whole lot of other stuff) do. Be sure you've got the right one. Check the speakers the same way I just told you to check your printer.

If your speakers plug directly into the wall without one of them power supply doodads, then be careful if you decide to go poking around inside them. Line current (that's what they call the stuff that comes out of the wall sockets) will kill you.

Sometimes the wires on your speakers will get wankulated and the speakers will quit working as a result. Check the wires, wiggle the connections, whatever.

Be sure your speakers are plugged into the correct jack on your sound card or motherboard. Check to verify that your speakers are turned on before doing any of this. If you're not sure about what's going on with the sound card, plug the speaker plug into every single hole that the little plug fits neatly inside of. The one that works is the one you should be using. Take a magic marker and make a black spot next to it so that the next time you move your stuff around and have to unplug the speakers for some reason, you can put the little plug back into the correct hole.

Other than that, there's not much you can do with your speakers.

There's nothing to see here. Move along.

Microphones

Voice recognition software doesn't.
Your computer is not a tape recorder.
Next subject please.

Cameras

You can just forget about fixing a digital camera. Read your owner's manual, despite the fact that it was written by pointy-headed idiots from the engineering, accounting, and legal departments. (See what I wrote back in the beginning of this thing to get a proper appreciation of those people.) I don't know how to run your camera. That's *your* job.

Ancient cameras can plug into your computer using your serial port or even your parallel port. You'll need the software that came with them to make your computer look around and discover that there's a camera out there. Needless to say, you'll need all the cables and disks and crap that came with the camera. Lose any of it and you're dead in the water, which is why people sometimes give these things away. Stuff the camera in a hole somewhere if the missing piece is hardware. You'll probably never encounter the weirdie little missing doodad, but if you do, you're all set to go. Software can sometimes be found on the Internet for download. Good luck—you'll need it.

Aside from that, it all boils down to the little USB connection that your camera uses to talk to your computer.

If your computer doesn't have the little rectangular hole that USB uses, you're gonna have to get a USB card to drop into one of the expansion slots on your motherboard. The card will have a rectangular hole or four that you can plug the camera into.

Your computer is supposed to be able to automagically discover the USB card and self-configure to suit. This usually happens like it's supposed to. If it doesn't happen, you're just plainly and simply outta luck. Nothing you can do with that computer/card combo. Go get another machine and try your luck with that one instead.

Your camera almost always comes with an installation CD. Do your best to *not* use this piece of crap, OK?

If your computer can find the camera when it's plugged into the USB port (please don't make me have to remind you to turn the camera on), then you can get to the pictures in the camera without having to use the messed-up installation CD's messed-up program. That installation CD is just loaded with spyware, adware, and Bob knows what else. It'll bog your machine down by hogging your memory, and it will load itself into memory *every single time you turn your computer on* until you learn how to type "msconfig" at your run prompt and then go in and rip all that rubbish out by the roots. You really oughtta be going into your registry, but I'm not gonna get into that little rant just this minute.

Get a proper image-handling program and load it into your machine and then diddle around with your pictures using that, even if it's the stunted little piece of junk that came with your OS.

Scanners

They usually come in two flavors: old and new. Old ones plug into your parallel port on the back of the computer and sit directly between your computer and your printer on the same line. New ones are USB.

Scanners require device drivers, and these files are sometimes found on your OS, sometimes found on a CD that came with the scanner, and sometimes have to be Googled up on the Internet and downloaded from there.

Scanner installation CDs are just as evil as anything else's installation CD, and if you can avoid it, then by all means do so. Lots of image manipulation software will be able to find your scanner and do just fine with it and not require the installation software that your scanner supposedly requires. Look for "twain" stuff on your menu under file/import or somewhere like that.

Imaging software is ridiculously overcomplex these days. Sorta like word processors. There's way too many options and ways to get lost just looking for a damn picture fer chrissakes! I can't give you a tutorial on this stuff; you've got to do it yourself. Ask a friend if you need to. Hit the Internet and find a discussion group that's not overrun with jerks who will whack you with RTFM (Read The F***ing Manual) every chance they get just to prove how much smarter they are than you. These people have no social skills. Find somebody who *does*.

Excepting the traveling scan head, scanners are remarkably simple devices consisting of a box with a glass lid and a hinged cover that goes over that. Sometimes the hinged cover is attached to little pin things that simply drop down into holes in the box. Lift up on the pins and the whole hinged cover comes right off in your hands.

Oftentimes people give scanners away because something bad has happened to the plate glass you set your item to be scanned down upon, and everything that gets scanned comes out with a bunch of lines and blurs on it.

However you do it, get to that glass lid and remove it. A surprising amount of times, you'll discover that some lint or mystery crud has managed to get smeared on the underside of the glass. So clean it off! Duh.

Alcohol and optical wipes are best for cleaning glass. If something weird is on the glass, get the something-weird cleaner and use it instead. Never *ever* use any abrasive to clean the glass. If the glass is scratched, you can bet your bottom dollar that it got that way because the previous owner of the scanner used Comet or Brillo pads to clean the glass with, or was in the habit of coming back from surfing and failing to clean the sand off his gritty little fingers before he started scanning stuff. Once the glass is scratched, that's it—no going back. Find out where the scratches are and put stuff over on the other side of the scanner when you need to get a shot of something. There's nothing else you can do except replace the glass, and that ain't cheap.

If the scanner immediately lints back up on the underside of the glass, consider removing the glass once again and then taking a bit of compressed air and blowing out the innards of the box. I have no idea what this lint *is* and how it gets inside the box, but if it's there and it keeps getting stirred up, blast it out of there and be done with it. Just don't go using the 100 psi nozzle from an inch away, 'cause you'll destroy the innards of the scanner.

If it keeps linting up anyway, consider moving it to a room where they're not shaping surfboard blanks or otherwise creating endless clouds of dust.

Game Stuff

Never touch it.

Rant on Computer Games

I suppose, before I start frothing at the mouth, that I should express my *deepest* appreciation for those idio . . . nice people who play computer games. Without these guys, my free computer would most likely be quite a bit more primitive than it is, and I'm well aware of that fact.

But there's no way in hell you're ever going to convince me that games are an appropriate thing to be doing with a device so marvelous as a computer! For my money, computers may as well be a gift from some wildly advanced spacefaring civilization that mistakenly left one behind here on Earth.

Computers DO things. And spectacularly incredible things at that!

Computers can calculate the orbits of satellites in conjunction with the precise orientation of this whirling globe in relation to the sun, allowing me to walk out into the backyard on a fine summer evening and stare in slack-jawed amazement as a canister full of humans glides serenely through the heavens, as unto a bright star, at the impossible-to-appreciate speed of 5 miles per *second*, even as still more computers keep the canister full of humans nice and safe inside.

Computers can slave away for endless hours and days,

checking thousands of inputs per second, just to make sure something that really better work, works.

Computers can fly airplanes better than Chuck Yeager.

Computers can accurately predict molecular interactions of as-yet-unmade chemicals, just to see if they might make your sore throat feel better. Or perhaps fix them damned Ebola viruses to where they're not quite the bother that they presently have become.

Computers can produce the sweetest sounds this side of heaven and then allow you to save and reproduce those sounds with flawless fidelity.

Computers are worthy devices. To use such a device to mindlessly entertain some idiot who's never heard of Richard Feynman strikes me as sheerest lunacy!

Fortunately for the idiots, I'm not in charge of anything.

And so they not only get to play the game but they also get to bitch and whine about how the computer they're using doesn't render the game as well as they'd like it to. Rendering is a most very mathematical task. The dork doing the whining is having trouble with 6 x 5 = __ and yet feels entitled to vent his wrath at the mathematical abilities of a machine. (Do NOT laugh! This actually happened to me at work just a week ago with a game-kiddy coworker.) There's enough irony in that to pick it up with a magnet, but the game kiddies don't really do irony very well either.

Come to think of it, these goofs don't do *ANYTHING* very well. And I'm guessing that it's because they're spending all that time in front of a game console, shooting virtual targets with a virtual gun in an attempt to get the virtual girl (the only girl these dorks will *ever* have a chance with).

What's behind it all? The megacorporations are all too aware that there's always going to be a need for warm bodies to take your order at McDogfood's, get you that pack of Marlboros at the 7-Eleven, or perhaps take out the trash from their own obscenely furnished offices. These warm bodies must be produced by the millions. The best way to keep the warm bodies stupid and submissive is to entertain them, because as long as they're being entertained, they're not *learning* anything. Not only that, for as long as they're being entertained, they're not going to be going outside in a frenzied mob to start burning large objects.

The big corporations know exactly how soon things become passé with the low-attention-span set and are therefore always looking for the next thing. With TV, movies, and music, it's more or less a matter of finding a new act, shilling it, and then sitting back and raking in the money. Computer games don't quite work that way. Or at least not yet they don't. What really drives the industry is an ever-increasing desire for fidelity of presentation. More realistic explosions and blood, more complicated story lines, and spiffier graphics to wow the ignoramuses.

The corporations must produce a better product with each passing year just to keep the dolts from wandering off somewhere in a daze and perhaps walking out into traffic or something. The "better product" demands a *better computer* to run it.

Last year's hot ticket is this year's, you guessed it, free computer!

And so, in a malignantly twisted way, computer games are actually GOOD. At least as long as you have the minimal intelligence to stay the hell away from playing the infernal things.

Take the cast-off machines that the gamers wouldn't be caught dead being seen with and give thanks to the Gods of Idiocy for providing you with not only a free computer but also some zombie at the McDogfood's to hand you your burger and fries.

Weirdie External Stuff

Yes indeed, I still come across some of those old 14.4 external modems. Laugh if you will, but if you're desperate and there's nothing else lying around, you will hook that sucker up and use it.

I've got a few of these kicking around in the pile and for

folks who only want e-mail, guess what? They work just
fine. The dolts who insist upon putting us in their personal
spam lists so they can send us idiotic stuff always wonder
why the folks with the 14.4 modems never reply or even
acknowledge receipt of this crap. It's because with a modem
that slow, any large file simply gets deleted prior to download. The owners of this ancient equipment know that
there's nothing in there for them, and so they just toss it.
I've put more than a few "friends" on my block sender list
after they refused to take me off their personal spam lists.
Screw that.

Anyhoo, Cro-Magnon external modems can occasionally
have a proper use and might even bail your sorry ass out of
a serious hole some fine lightning-infested summer day.
Don't throw 'em out. Give 'em to old folks who only want e-
mail from Juno or something like that.

Until quite recently, I was the owner of a bizarre 1x
external CD drive that hooked to the machine via the printer port. Weird as all hell and twice as slow, but for laptops
without CD drives, it oftentimes was the only way to get an
OS onto the hard drive. That thing really came through in
the clutch over the years, and I only recently reluctantly
gave it the last rites and chucked it. Thanks, Sprocket, for
the little Autobahn CD drive. I owe you a couple of nice
waves for that thing.

In general, bizarro external doodads require bizarro
device drivers in particular and software in general. Don't
plan on getting something in this category complete with
the disks it came with. Neither should you throw it away
after not being able to find the damn programs after a year
and a half of looking. Sure as you toss it, the software will
fall out of the sky into your lap the next week. The above-
mentioned Autobahn CD drive is gone, but the software still
resides on several hard drives. Can't ever tell if another one
will fall out of the sky on me, eh? If there's anybody out
there with one of these things and no software to run it,
contact me via Paladin Press and I'll shoot you a copy. Fits

easily on a 1.4-MB floppy and only involves a couple of tweaks to autoexec.bat and config.sys. Nothing to it.

Externals run with external power. We've covered that already, yes?

Weird cables for weird externals are never to be trusted. That goofy-looking wire is just as old as the weirdo external it's hooking to your machine. We've already talked more than enough about wires, haven't we? You know what needs to be done.

Let's go talk about software, OK? I'm sick of all this clunky junk lying around all over the place.

Chapter 4

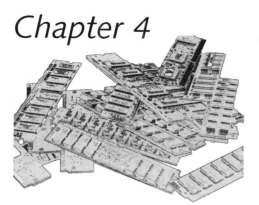

Software

Without it, computers don't work.
Guess we better check into it, hmm?

OPERATING SYSTEMS

Your OS (yep, that's what that means: operating system) is the cerebral cortex of your computing system. Computers, like certain people I know, can run without the use of a cerebral cortex, but they don't really DO much. Other things are equally vital to maintaining your computer's homeostasis, but without the OS it's all pretty pointless.

Your OS is the central clearinghouse for operating all those applications you've crammed onto your hard drive. It keeps everybody running smoothly and keeps 'em from bumping into each other and turning your finely tuned system into the great train wreck. It's a mind-bogglingly large and complicated set of interlocking doojiggers and deely-boppers, and when it gets a little out of whack, it once again mimics a cerebral cortex—only this time the cerebral cortex is owned by a crazy guy and weird things come out of it all the time for no real reason.

OS developers have been attempting to hone their products ever since the inception of the computer back in Cambrian times, but they still haven't gotten it totally right. Computers are still just a little bit nuts, and if you stroke them in exactly the right way, they can become full-blown paranoid schizophrenics with blatant homicidal tendencies. Unfortunately for us all, we really don't quite know what "exactly the right way" consists of at all times, and an eruption of lunacy is always just a mouse click or a keystroke away. Bad things just sort of happen and the screen goes kerplunk and that's that.

Everybody's OS crashes at one time or another, despite what the disciples of the One True Path (such as those Linux penguinoids) may attempt to persuade you about how wonderful their particular version of computing heaven is.

Enough of this rubbish. Where's the OS?

BIOS

The BIOS: It's not a *real* operating system, but an incredible soy substitute!

Or something like that.

Actually, your BIOS is like a little mini operating system, a sort of homunculus of an operating system wired right into the physical atoms of your computer's motherboard. It allows the silicon-hearted beast to kind of wake up, gain a dim awareness of its surroundings, and then immediately go over and kick the *real* operating system to wake it up and get it to go to work doing all that swell stuff it's making the big bucks to do.

An OS for your OS, if you will.

Whatever it is, it's for damn sure that if it's not working, or it's working within a drug-induced nebula of wrongly advised electrons, you don't have a computer. Period.

Your BIOS is what runs your POST (power-on self test)

to see what's out there and whether or not it's working like it should.

If your BIOS can't find your memory, your computer *has* no memory.

If your BIOS can't find your hard drives, your computer *has* no hard drives.

If your BIOS is delusional about anything and is given to expect to see things that aren't there, there *are* no things there.

Getting the idea here yet? Fair to partly important item, your BIOS is.

For good or for bad, your BIOS is *adjustable*. Adjust it right, and all's well with the world. Adjust it wrong, and there be great gnashing of teeth far and wide across the land.

BIOS comes with a set of defaults that will instantly replace whatever you put in their place the nanosecond your CMOS battery goes dead or gets removed from its little holder on the motherboard. Oftentimes, the defaults your BIOS reverts to will cause you to wonder which planet exactly did its inventors come from, and was it a planet from the Milky Way or perhaps some more distant galaxy?

Every computer I've ever seen seems to do just fine with BIOS settings that say "auto" for any soft or hard drive. Why, then, am I always stumbling across defaults that read "none" for any soft or hard drive? None, to my way of thinking, is none, and if the computer thinks it has *none* floppy or hard or CD drives, then it's gonna by god shrug its shoulders and most very reasonably stop dead in its tracks just as soon as it makes that discovery. (This is a clue as to how stupid computers really are. You or I, if hooked up to a couple of hard drives, would immediately notice that salient fact upon waking up, despite being told by the guy standing right next to us, "No, there are no hard drives hooked up to you." Your computer, on the other hand, actually believes this guy and commences to utterly fail to perceive the fact that "Yes, there really are a couple of hard drives wired directly to my ass, no matter what that guy is saying.")

Your BIOS is very persuasive, and if it gets something wrong, the whole house of cards promptly collapses and stays that way until something is done to teach your BIOS the error of its ways.

I just went through this with a new CD burner two days ago when I spent an entire day futilely attempting to get this bastard to go and having no luck at all! I entered the machine's BIOS looking for an entirely different thing when I discovered that I was rigged for primary master: auto; primary slave: auto; secondary master: auto; secondary slave: none. None, *none, NONE!* Arrrrggghhhh!!!!!

How the hell my BIOS ever got that way, I'm sure I'll never know. Here I am, the guy who's writing the damned book on it, and I *still* managed to foul it up!!!

Set secondary slave to "auto" and all of a sudden I've got a new CD burner. Well sorta. There's actually additional problems that I'll share with you here a bit later on.

Wipes froth from corners of mouth.

OK, where was I?

Oh yeah, the BIOS.

Anything that connects to the motherboard using those IDE ribbon cables is directly controlled by the BIOS. Set all four items (primary master, primary slave, secondary master, secondary slave in case you've forgotten) to auto and leave it alone thenceforth.

For some weird reason the BIOS will occasionally up and decide to reset itself to some damned thing or other (and most definitely not always the default settings), and whatever is on that particular circuit will promptly quit working or merely start working with a very poor attitude. My above debacle of two days ago included my machine's OS actually discovering the damn CD drive and half-assedly accessing it (enough to mislead me, not enough to actually work) once in a while just to see if it could make me look even stupider than I already am.

When you first power up your computer, you'll get a little message along the lines of "Press del to enter setup, esc to skip memory test" somewhere on that black screen with the white printing that shows up immediately upon powering the machine up. (Del means the "delete" key and esc means the "escape" key. Skipping the memory test can take a few seconds off your boot-up time.) If this flickers by too fast to read, whack the "pause" key as soon as it pops up. That'll freeze it for as long as it takes you to copy down the required magic keystroke(s). Hit "enter" or the space bar to kick the machine back to life when you're done copying this stuff down on paper. Shutting the machine off with a flick of the power switch (or even snatching the wire from the wall socket) won't hurt a thing if done before the POST routine finishes up and the *real* OS starts shuddering to life. However, once the Big Guy has started showing signs of life, it's best to let it come all the way to the surface before shutting it back off.

Entering setup is how you adjust your BIOS, and different BIOS manufacturers have different magic keystrokes to accomplish this. Some of 'em go an additional step to make things difficult by splashing your screen with their logo, thus hiding the POST screen as the POST is doing its thing. This also hides any required instructions for entering setup, leaving you to guess wrongly at it or go find out how it's done by asking somebody or maybe Googling for it. Sometimes F1 does it. Or perhaps F10. Or maybe ctrl-alt-esc (hold down ctrl and alt, and then tap esc). There are more ways to enter setup than this, but you're getting the idea. Delete seems to be the most popular, but it's by no means any kind of "standard."

Once inside the setup screen(s) it's time to be very careful. Flub this stuff up, and you can wind up chasing your tail around the living room for an amazing amount of time, or even wind up wrongly believing that the computer is broken for real.

Before we actually go inside the setup screen, there's one more thing I want to warn you about: flash BIOS. BIOS worked just fine and dandy for years and years, so of course they decided that it needed fixing. What they came up with is a BIOS that can be flashed, which means that the atoms get sort of rearranged in there in way that allows the newly flashed BIOS to retain its new settings even though the dog ate your CMOS battery. Think of it as adjustable default settings for your BIOS, and you won't be far wrong as to the sense of the thing. Or maybe think of it as a way to add new and better settings in your BIOS that you can now adjust with glee, whereas before you were stuck with whatever the computer gave you and that's that.

Only problem with flashing a BIOS is that . . . well, wait a minute here, there's actually *two* problems with flashing a BIOS.

The first and most obvious problem is that it introduces an additional layer of crap you have to go through and perhaps mess up and have to backtrack from, wasting hours and hours of otherwise useful time spent working on a computer. Once you can get to your setup screen, there's no reason to go fooling around with the innards of your BIOS by flashing it. Waste of time.

The second reason is more important, however. Mess up a BIOS flash and you may well have thoroughly wrecked your computer in a way that is in no way different from dropping it over the side of a cruise ship that's in water a couple of miles deep. Splash, and it's gone. Once done properly wrong, it can *never* be undone. Flounder a flash and you just might have fixed things so that your computer will never again be able to talk or listen to you via things like monitors, keyboards, floppy drives, and pretty much anything else. Once your computer has entered this sort of catatonic state, there's no way you can *ever* get any more information into it! (Like, say, perhaps a second attempt at flashing the BIOS.) Game, set, match! You lose!

On machines that are just a step away from the trash pile, by all means flash away, baby! Nothing to lose, right? Find out what flavor the motherboard is and whether the BIOS is even flashable or not and then download the files and load them puppies up. What the hell, why not?

For machines that are already working well enough and that you'd like to keep on using with the same motherboard still inside, perhaps you'd best be a trifle more careful about things like flashing a BIOS. In fact, perhaps you'd best not do it at all, hmm?

Setup Screen

The setup screen is where you can diddle your BIOS to your heart's content, but like I said earlier, be careful in there!

You really need to know your way around in here because an amazing amount of free computers will come your way with apologies from their owners regarding their brokenness, and then you'll go in and discover that all that's wrong is that the damned setup was all flonked-up. This almost always happens after the owner has dropped a grand or three on a new machine, so there's hardly ever any worries about giving any of it back, even after you tell the doof owner that his rig was just ticky-boo. Most times folks don't want to be told this stuff at all, owing to worries on their part about being made to look stupid. Why these goofs are more worried about *looking* stupid as opposed to worrying about *being* stupid is not for me to know. Or care.

The main menu page for your setup will have a list that can run to over a dozen discrete categories of stuff to mangle, each with its own dozens of sub, and occasional sub-submenus.

Try not to mangle any more stuff than is humanly possible. You go screwing with one of these things the wrong way and it can cause your machine to quit running. Doofy things like "Memory Hole At 15Mb Addr." are things you should be laying the hell off of. What's a memory hole anyway? Who knows? Who cares? Is the machine running reasonably well? Then leave the thing alone, OK? (Just for the record, my memory hole at 15Mb addr. is disabled, and since the machine works just fine that way, I fully intend to leave it disabled. You should too.)

One of the things you do want to check into and tweak if needed is your "Standard CMOS Setup," which is where you're gonna be telling the machine that Drive A is a 1.44 MB, 3.5-inch floppy and every last one of them four hard disks are going to be type: auto. If you'd like to set the date while you're in here, then fine, go right ahead. I like to use software (nistime-32bit.exe does just fine for keeping me within a second or so of official atomic clock time) for that but it's not mandatory.

Something else to check is BIOS features setup, where things like boot sequence can be twiddled with. (Please keep in mind that different BIOS call this stuff by different names. Hunt around till you find something that looks like what I'm talking about, OK? Use your street smarts.) Occasionally, a BIOS will need to be changed to permit you to boot off of a CD, and then changed right back to allow you to boot normally from a hard drive; otherwise, it will whine and pout and advise you to "insert boot media" into your damned CD drive. CDs are good to boot off of when loading a new OS; otherwise, they're something you should only invoke when you feel like invoking them. (Gimme a minute here and we'll get to "autoplay," I promise.) Most BIOS will skip right over an empty CD drive and boot off the hard drive like they're supposed to, but not all of 'em. It's the sneaky things like this that will trip you up, time and time again.

Typematic rate is something you might wanna fool around with. For me, the cursor never moves fast enough to the right or left when I hold down one of them arrow keys, and I have to juice up the typematic rate to its fastest setting in my BIOS with each new machine I fire up.

Boot up numlock status is another favorite of mine. I like it set to "on."

There's more, but I don't want to spoil all the fun by droning on and on with this stuff.

Play with this stuff all you want to, but don't go playing with too much of it at the same time. Change one item, then reboot the machine to see if it works. If it don't work, reboot again and enter setup and change that one item back to whatever it was set at before you got itchy keyfingers and went in there and doodled around with it.

The more you do this, the more you'll come to understand what's OK to play with and what's to be left well enough alone. Keep at it—the exercise will do you good.

Should you wreck the train and be unable to get it back on track, you do have a bit of breathing room to wiggle in. Enter setup and find something that says "load defaults" and invoke that. This *should* (note the careful choice of words there, please) allow your machine to come back to enough of a life to let you then go into things like your BIOS defaults and reset all those hard disks back to auto once again.

If you can't even get a proper screen to show up and therefore can't go pressing keys in a vain hope that something—anything—might work, you can always power the machine off, take the CMOS battery out of it, and then let it sit there for a good little while. Let them capacitors bleed off every last electron they're holding onto. Overnight is best, but sometimes things happen instantly, the second that little battery pops out of its socket. Then put the CMOS battery back in and fire up the rig. With luck, you'll be back on the system defaults. Go from there, as described above.

Stuff like that.

Something else to be extra careful with is the password stuff. I leave it alone unless it's my machine. Remembering passwords is something with zero tolerance for screwups. You forget the password, your computer forgets how to boot up. No fun there.

Enjoy your little walk through the Enchanted Forest. Just don't go leaving a trail of bread crumbs to find your way back home, OK?

PARTITIONING, FORMATTING, AND THAT KIND OF THING

Welcome to the land of chicken and egg. Which came

first, your OS or the partitioning and formatting that allows it to be loaded and run?

Generally speaking, the OS has to be around somewhere to permit you to partition and format, but since the OS cannot be loaded without said partitioning and formatting, my guess is that the egg came first and then the chicken followed. Eggs apparently were carved onto floppy disks using stone tools and primitive fire, thus allowing us to enter the new millennium with a shiny OS that will make our computer sing and dance just the way we want it to.

Or something. When firing up a freebie rig, many, many times the damned thing won't go. Or will only go just a little way before it sulls up and quits.

If the BIOS successfully finds your hard drive, the very next step is to check to see if the hard drive is partitioned and formatted the way it's supposed to be. If the BIOS can't even find the hard drive (please check them settings again and make sure they're set to auto), then you're outta luck. Put that particular hard drive on the shelf and leave it there for a month or so. If you're really lucky, the BIOS will find it the next time you do this. But even if it does, it's at death's door; after you extract such information off it as behooves you to, you can more or less plan on taking it apart to play with as opposed to using it for any sensible tasks.

I highly recommend having a Windows 98 boot disk lying around. These little jobbers are handy as hell when poking around in an unknown machine. A Linux boot disk is also very handy, but not nearly as handy as Bill Gates' little creation. This is because for every machine you discover to be loaded (however crippledly) with Linux, you'll discover about ten thousand loaded with some form of Windows.

Welcome to reality, children, we've been expecting you.

How to Use Fdisk

Alright, enough of this. Let's go play with fdisk. Not a misspelling there, fdisk it is.

There are times you will need to find out if your problem is a busted hard drive or merely a hard drive that doesn't quite have its head together software-wise. For example, you may boot up your machine and, after the POST screens go by, you may see either nothing at all or dire warnings such as "insert boot disk," "press a key to reboot," or "disk boot failure insert system disk and press enter."

Enter fdisk. (Oh, by the way, just in case you're really stupid, I suppose I oughtta tell you right now that if your hard drive spins right up and delivers a properly operating OS, then lay off with the fdisk, OK? Fdisk giveth, and fdisk taketh away. And when fdisk taketh away, it taketh *away*. Poof! Everything's gone.)

Put your handy-dandy Windows 98 boot disk into drive A and turn the machine on. If W98 isn't your OS, then get one of your spare hard drives that does have it and replace your regular drive with the one that has W98. Fire it up, hit the start button on the Windows desktop, go to help, go to the search part of help, and type "startup disk" into the little space they give you. Whack the enter key and it'll give you some choices. Down at the bottom of the list it'll say: "To create a startup disk." Double click on that guy and all of a sudden it's telling you the tale. Follow the instructions and make the disk. If you can't do any of the above, then go bum one from a buddy, or have said buddy make one using *his* W98 machine per what I just wrote above.

Be sure the floppy drive is write protected after you have turned it into your Windows 98 boot disk. Oftentimes dead hard drives get that way because a virus infected them and wiped them out. As long as your floppy is write protected (both little holes on the top corners of the floppy are open for light to shine right through), the virus can't get on it and cause further trouble. Remove all additional hard drives from the machine too. Same deal with the viruses, but since you can't write protect a hard drive while you're doing this, you simply remove it.

When it asks, tell it you don't want "CD-ROM support";

bootup goes faster that way. When you finally see a little
"A:\ >" deal, you're ready to go. Type in "fdisk" and then
whack enter.

If the drive is bigger than 500 MB, it will ask you if
you'd like to enable large disk support (Y/N).........? [Y] Just
whack the enter key here and give it not a moment's additional thought. (I'm not gonna keep on with this "whack
enter" stuff. By now, you should already know that's how
things happen. You also know not to type in the quotation
marks around all these terms, right?)

If the hard drive is *smaller* than 500 MB, you don't get this
screen—it goes immediately to a list of choices you can make:

1. Create DOS partition or Logical DOS Drive
2. Set active partition
3. Delete partition or Logical DOS Drive
4. Display partition information

If you have more than one hard drive, you have to
invoke choice 5, which asks which drive you want to look
at. Do this if you have to, but I strongly urge you to remove
everything except the drive you're interested in checking
here. Pull the ribbon cable out of any drive that you know
already works just fine and dandy; that way you can't fry it
with fdisk. Remove it physically from the machine if that
makes you feel any better or safer here. If you instruct
fdisk to go to the wrong drive and further instruct it to
remove things like partitions, it will eradicate everything on
that drive with a smile on its face and then ask for more.
YOU HAVE BEEN WARNED!

If you've had to disconnect a second (or even third or
fourth!) hard drive, you'll have to reset the jumpers on the
hard drive you're now playing with solo in order to let the
machine know it's now just a single drive. Go back and read
the section on hard drives again if you need to and pay double extra close attention to the "jumpers" part this time and
you'll be fine.

Choice 4 is the one we want here. Choices 1, 2, and 3 are a waste of time, and choice 3 is also a great way to erase everything and ruin your whole day. Be careful with things like "Delete partition or Logical DOS Drive," OK?

Choice 4 will "Display partition information" and that's exactly what we want, so do it.

If there's no partition (this would explain a dead machine immediately following a "operating system not found" message at bootup), you'll get a mostly blank screen and down near the bottom it will say, "No partitions defined." If this happens, press escape and invoke choice 1. Skip on down below in this part till you get to "Create DOS partition or Logical DOS Drive" and follow what it says to do. You'll be fine and you'll also be glad because you saved yourself a whole lot of diddling around with stuff.

If there's *something* in there, this will come up next:

Partition	Status	Type	Volume Label	Mbytes	System	Usage

Underneath each one of them may or may not be some information.

If you get something like this:

Partition	Status	Type	Volume Label	Mbytes	System	Usage
C: 1	A	PRI DOS		820	FAT32	100%

You're in deep doo-doo because everything is just fine and the damn thing still doesn't work, which probably means that the hard drive itself is FUBAR. I've got exactly this staring at me from my backup machine right this second, and since this is not the first time I've played around with it, I can assure you that the hard drive in question is kaput.

What appears below the headers I've just shown you can vary wildly. If what shows up under "system" is "unknown," you may have a functioning partition, but the Win98 disk will be unable to deal with it. Weirdie operating systems can do this. Unix can do this. If they're not working (as in boot-

ing up to a sensible, *working* user interface), then there's no
reason not to nuke them. Nuking also applies if you've got
an OS that seems to work fine but stops cold when it asks
you for a password you don't have. You're dead in the water.
Nuke it!

Go ahead and "Press Esc to continue" like it says, and
since the damned partition that's there already doesn't
work for diddly (you've checked repeatedly, right?), you're
gonna nuke it. Go ahead and select the dreaded choice 3.
Why not?

Another set of choices appears, asking exactly what
you'd like to delete.

If it said "PRI DOS" under "type" on the previous set of
choices, go for choice 1 and "Delete Primary DOS Partition"
and be done with it.

Non-DOS partitions can be deleted using choice 4,
"Delete Non-DOS partition."

If you make a wrong choice, fdisk will immediately
inform you that no such partition exists, and you can then
pick another type of partition to delete until you get it right.

When you get it right, you get a flashing WARNING!
along with an admonition that data in the deleted partition
will be lost and yet another question regarding exactly what
partition you'd like to delete. If you're not sure what partition to delete at this point, read just above the warning
words and it will tell you everything you need to know.

Creating a Partition

Hard drives can come with a whole slew of different
partitions. Primary, extended, non-DOS, you name it. Most
of the time they'll only have one, and it will be primary
DOS, but not always. Not by any means. That's why you
should wipe them ALL out—just keep on invoking fdisk and
wiping them out till there's nothing left. Fill in the Volume
Label if it's required. (Read it from what's just above where
it's asking.) When they're all gone, fdisk choice 3, "Delete
partition or Logical DOS Drive," will yield a mostly blank

screen and that note near the bottom saying, "No partitions to delete."

Now we "Create DOS partition or Logical DOS Drive," which is fdisk's choice 1.

Make it primary and make it the maximum available size.

Formatting

Now it's almost time to shut the machine off momentarily. Be ready to *format* when you boot back up using your trusty Windows 98 startup disk. Partitioning is not enough; we *must* format, otherwise our operating system will not understand where we're attempting to place it. An unformatted hard drive is strictly *terra incognita* when it comes to operating systems. As before, with fdisk, if the damned thing works already, do not format it. Not required. Wipes every last bit of data from the hard drive. Drastic measure. Be careful with it.

Press esc to continue. You should be back to that "A:\>" deal.

Power switch to "off."

Let the hard drive spin down. Leave W98 boot disk in A drive. Power switch back to "on."

Start computer without CD-ROM support.

Back to the little "A:\>" deal.

Fdisk again and choice 4 again, just to see what happened.

System has become "unknown." Might already have been that way. Don't matter.

Press esc to continue.

Press esc to exit fdisk.

At the "A:\>", type "format c: /s" but only if the drive you're going to format is C drive. Don't go having additional hard drive(s) in the machine at this point. One hard drive *only*. The one you're working on. Only. You go formatting the wrong hard drive and you just lost *everything*.

Y for yes and proceed.

Now we wait while it formats. If it's a multi-gig drive (how'd you get *that*?), it's gonna take awhile. While we wait,

I'll explain what the little "/s" meant after the "format c:"
It's supposed to place the "system files" on the hard drive
and allow you to boot up from the newly formatted hard
drive to get a little "C:\>" deal after it boots. Won't do much
other than that, but I've found that if it will boot right up
with no problems following a format, it's a good sign that
the drive is healthy.

If, when the format finishes up, you get something like
"Format complete. Sector not found reading drive C Abort,
Retry, Ignore, Fail?" you're a dead duck. This is another
place where the little "/s" after the "format c:" comes in
handy. It forces an immediate file write to the disk following the format. When there's a problem writing a file (sector
not found, perhaps?), you're not gonna be happy.

Your drive's toast.

Now all that's left is to hit "I" repeatedly till it kicks all
the way through and you get the "A:\>" deal again.
Remove the floppy disk and boot the machine. Sorry,
bucko. If things had worked out right, it would have asked
you for a "Volume Label" at some point toward the very tail
end of things.

What It All Means

OK, all of the above (and there certainly was a lot of it,
wasn't there?) is more by way of example than it is by way
of hard and fast rules. Many, many times, your newly
acquired hard drive will flunk somewhere among the above
tests. It was free after all—what were you expecting? And
dead hard drives are one of the main reasons people think
they've got a dead computer; replace the hard drive and
you're ready to go.

But first you gotta test it, and I can hear screams of rage
coming from certain quarters out there telling all of us what
a stupid way this is to test hard drives.

In a way, they're right. But in reality, they're wrong.

We're just *learning* this stuff here, yes? And anything
that makes things simpler is a good thing. Fdisk is as simple

as it gets, although it WILL murder your data in an instant if you use it incorrectly.

Your Win98 machine also has something called "scandisk" in it, but I advise against using that. Damned thing takes *forever* if it goes into "surface scan" mode and, on top of that, if it finds bad spots on the drive and you agree to "fix it," it not only fails to fix anything but instead rips things out by the roots. Leave the surface scan out of it. Waste of time.

Specialty software to test your hard drive and spiff it up if necessary is just that: specialty software. Can be tricky to use and costs a buck or three. Assumes you're computer savvy, which you are not at this point. Later, maybe, but not now.

All we're looking for here is something quick and dirty that can actually do the job. Your Windows 98 boot disk will do the job of finding dead and dying hard drives right quick like.

Fdisk at least has the minimal sense to recognize a big, fat NTFS partition on a drive. If you see that, don't get hasty and go wiping it out and replacing it with FAT32 (this stuff will be self-evident when you fdisk, trust me).

If you get your hands on a large hard drive and can reasonably expect that some kind of damned thing like Windows 2000 or XP or whatever is on there, or at least it was partitioned and formatted that way, then my guess is that you're already running a program in that class.

In which case, jumper your found hard drive for primary slave, secondary master, or secondary slave. Hook it up to the machine you're running Windows XP on and then invoke "Administrative Tools." From in there, you click "Computer Management." In there, you click "Disk Management" and—hey, presto!—there's your drive all nice and easy to see. If it's wonkulated partition-wise, you'll know right away. Repartition and format if required. It's a breeze. And by the way, please notice that "fdisk" appears not at all in Windows XP-type situations.

Been swept under the rug. Wonder why?

When dealing with a dual-drive setup as described right above, be double damn sure that the main drive has virus protection. Wonky drives routinely get that way from viral infections. This is yet another reason I like doing things with a single hard drive and a write-protected floppy, which takes us right back to that damned Windows 98 boot disk again.

Windows XP will create a boot disk for you, yes indeed it will. But it won't *do* anything other than boot you into that "A:\>" dingdong. No fdisk, no nothing. Bill Gates and crew must have decided somewhere along the line that fdisk from a floppy was a no-no. Not sure how or why, but it sure the hell is. Thanks, guys.

One more little tidbit while we're at it here. Your hard drive has something on it called the "master boot record" and it's in a place that none of your (nonspecialized) software will ever touch. Should you be suspicious that a virus may be lurking there (viruses are VERY specialized software), you can do the fdisk thing a slightly different way: Instead of "fdisk" you type "fdisk /mbr" and proceed on your merry way. Fdisk /mbr won't even acknowledge that anything happened at all. You just go right back to that "A:\>" doodad as if nothing at all happened. What actually happened was that fdisk rewrote your master boot record and didn't bother to tell you that it did so. If a virus was in there, it got written over along with everything else. Kind of like getting run over by a bus. Unless, of course, as part of its viral program it loaded itself into memory and then promptly wrote itself right back into your master boot record as soon as fdisk was finished with it. These sorts of things do happen.

Partitioning and formatting are pretty good (but certainly not perfect) ways of exterminating viruses, but it's a scorched-earth policy. Everything, virus and all, goes down the flusher. None of this is a proper substitute for a virus-scanning program. There's free ones available for download.

I'm running AVG and it works just fine and has never let me down—so far. There's others too. Go get one and run it religiously, OK? Run a scanner for Trojans too. (Trojans are different and require different software to sniff them out. A lot of that stuff is free too.)

OK. The hard drive is checked out and it works. Can we go *do* something with it?

Yes we can.

FACE IT, BILL GATES OWNS THE ENTIRE WORLD

As you may or may not have gathered from the foregoing, we're talking about Microsoft products and how to run the damnable things. There's a reason for this.

Computers in general and free computers in particular can be counted on to run Microdork software with an expectation approaching 100 percent. And it's a pretty *close* approach to 100 percent in case you were wondering.

Gates and company are the robber barons for the new millennium and have maneuvered themselves into a monopoly position when it comes to the operating systems and major software programs that run on computers. Apple is running such a distant second that nobody can even see 'em except for other Applenoids. Linux is making a move, but since they're still behind Apple (for the moment, at least), they're also invisible on the landscape.

And no matter what happens in the near future with software and who has what when it comes to market share, it won't make a damn bit of difference for you and me and our free machines. People don't give away *new* computers. And you can bet your bottom dollar that that old machine you glom onto is going to have an *old* operating system and *old* major software. Read: Windows OS and MS Word, Excel, Outlook, Internet Explorer, and all the rest of that kind of stuff. This isn't going to be changing in the world of free computers for quite some time.

So we may as well not only get used to it but figure out how to take advantage of it, eh?

Right off the bat, the main advantage of the fact that Bill Gates owns the entire world is standardization. I can't say enough nice things about the fact that everybody, but everybody, is running the same OS. If you've paid the least attention throughout the first parts of this thing, you'll already have a fine appreciation of the fact that there's just about a zillion ways to put a computer together. This means the poor bastard who's attempting to fix the damned thing has to understand all zillion ways in order to be able to deal successfully with the bewildering array of contingencies that may come his way when the next machine shows up on the doorstep.

That sucks.

But with the ubiquity of Windows, we've arrived in a place where all you have to know is ONE system. Now the fact that the one system is more complicated and capable of throwing curves at you than an ex-wife certainly doesn't make matters any easier, but there's an awful lot of ways that things could be harder. So be glad that everybody is running Windows. Same set of nuts and bolts on every machine. Neat-o. Seen one, seen 'em all.

One of the main complaints that people have against Microswill is the horrendous price they're charging for that software of theirs, and it's a fair complaint. Hundreds of dollars for a stupid OS is completely out of the question.

But guess what, children? We're not paying a nickel for *any* of it. We're getting it for free with our free machines. Once you take the price gouging out of the equation, then all of a sudden things start to look quite a bit nicer. Microrip quits being a rip. Hell, all of a sudden it's a damned give-away! And it's really nice stuff too. All slick and shiny with every bell and whistle you could ask for.

Cool, huh?

This, then, is another advantage we can take of the fact

that Bill Gates owns the whole world. His products have gotten so plentiful that we can get them for *nothing*. *Microsoft software is free software.*

Why That's a Good Thing

Because it's absolutely everywhere, older stuff like Windows 98 is just lying around on the ground waiting for you to pick it up. The disks are a dime a dozen. Installation keys can be Googled for with every expectation of getting a good key. Windows 98 is worth having merely for the start-up disk you can make with it. Fdisk is a powerful tool that nobody should be without.

The fact that things can be made to run from a floppy cannot be oversold either. Many's the time, when working with an ancient machine that's having major problems, that the only way to get the damned thing to go is to boot off of a floppy and then invoke hard drives and CD drives from there.

Learn what a command prompt is. It's that funny "A:\>" thing I was talking about a few minutes ago. When it's done from your hard drive, it looks like "C:\>" instead. Or even "D:\>" or "E:\>" or a few other letters in the first part of the alphabet if you've got more than one hard drive and perhaps if one or all of 'em have compressed disks.

Type in "c:" and enter it. (Again, no quotes, please.) One hard drive only, please.

Here we are, downtown at "C:\>."

Now let's go in there and have a little look around inside. Type "dir" and hit enter and see what happens. You'll get a list of stuff. Some of it is files, and some of it is directories. The files are just files, but the directories will contain files and even more directories, and this can go on in a chain for quite a ways sometimes.

Poke around in there. If the list looks something like this, your hard drive is probably fair to partly OK at least to a first approximation:

```
C:\ > dir
Volume in drive C is DORA_LIVES
Volume Serial Number is 1C7D-1C09
Directory of C:\

AUTOEXEC   BAT                0      06-21-02      10:51p
COMMAND COM             93,880      05-11-98       8:01p
CONFIG     SYS               0      06-07-03       9:40p
MYDOCU ~ 1      < DIR >             06-30-02       9:00p
NETLOG     TXT           6,066      06-21-02      10:50p
PROGRA ~ 1      < DIR >             06-30-02       9:00p
SCANDISK   LOG          1,399      06-30-02      12:27a
WINDOWS         < DIR >             06-30-02       8:55p
WINDOW ~ 1      < DIR >             06-30-02       9:00p
          5 file(s)    101,345 bytes
          4 dir(s)106,012,672 bytes free
```

This data shows that your hard drive *at least* has the
minimal sense to advise you that it has five *files* and four
directories on it. The files are just files, the directories may
contain Bob knows what, in a seemingly endless labyrinth
of descending subdirectories, sub-subdirectories, and on and
on, with each step along the way fully capable of being
plastered wall to wall with a zillion files of any size, shape,
or color.

I'm gonna stop right here with this stuff. I will only
advise you that there's a whole world of commands and
arcane syntax that you can invoke to discover what's on a
hard drive. And this is without ever having the thing boot
itself up or slaving it to some other master drive and pray-
ing that it isn't infected with some kind of dire virus that
will immediately go and infect your good drive.

If you like digging for dirt, this is just one of the alterna-
tive ways to do it while minimizing the chances of getting
something nasty all over yourself. But really, it's pretty
much enough to know that the thing works. Who cares
what's on it? Does it work? Well then, let's wipe it clean and

put a new OS on it along with some applications software
and then get back to the business of giving it away.

The next step along the Windows Way is the installation
CD. If the hard drive boots but has some ancient stuff on it
like Windows 3.1, then just as soon as you've booted it successfully, you can skip all the foregoing and simply put an
installation CD in the drive and install a better version of
Windows. Unless, of course, you wish to go through the pre-
existing contents of the hard drive with a fine-toothed comb
in search of . . . whatever might be lurking there. When
you're done peeking into all the nooks and crannies, then
you can whip out the installation CD, OK? Suit yourself on
this one, folks. The call is entirely your own.

Back to the installation CD.

To begin with, you've gotta *have* one, yes?

Getting an installation CD used to be a bit of a problem.
Fortunately, that's no longer the case. With the incredible
cheapness of blank CDs and the ubiquity of CD burners on
most computers now, things couldn't be easier when it
comes to getting your hands on an installation CD.

Get in touch with the college kids I talked about waaaay
back in the beginning of this thing. Those guys just *love* to
burn copies of installation CDs for their friends. Don't forget to bring your social skills with you, OK? Frumpy old
Republicans with closed minds and open mouths aren't
going to get very far with the guys in the computer lab
when it comes to asking for favors.

But even if you *are* a frumpy old Republican and all you
know is a whole crowd of other frumpy old Republicans,
you really don't have to worry. Republicans like stealing
things just as much as bearded collegians. More even. Ask
the Republican of your choice to burn you a copy of his
installation CD, and dollars to donuts says that he'll cheerfully do so.

Windows 95 and 98 disks can be had for nothing with a
free computer a surprising amount of times. Beware the
dreaded OEM (original equipment manufacturer) disks,

though. These things have been specially tweaked to only install on a certain manufacturer's machine; with the wrong type of machine, you're out of luck—the damned thing won't work. This also applies to newer versions of Windows. Right this minute, I'm the proud possessor of a Windows ME installation disk, but I don't have the only damned machine it is compatible with. Damn you, Toshiba! I'm gonna hang on to it anyway, 'cause one fine day I just might *need* the thing to repair somebody's Toshiba machine or maybe I'll glom onto one and be able to use it that way. Never underestimate the power of useless software to suddenly become critical for some weird-assed reason one day. More on that in a minute.

Higher level versions of Windows than 98 have also become surprisingly easy to come by. Bill Gates and his evil minions have become enraged at this turn of events, but there's really very little that they can do about it. At least for now.

Another wiggle in the installation CD saga is the "upgrade" versions as opposed to the standard start-from-scratch versions. Basically, if you've got an upgrade installation CD, the first thing it does is look on your hard drive to see if a previous version of Windows is already there, so it can "upgrade" it. No previous version, no upgrade. And sometimes the "from scratch" versions won't work when they *do* find a previous version. Google on the Internet to see what to do when that happens. A file named "WIN.COM" (among a few other things) will be in there somewhere if I'm not mistaken. For the upgrade problem, you basically want to have a set of ancient installation floppies lying around. I've got Windows 3.1 *and* 95 floppies. I take good care of them. When I need to upgrade somebody's hard drive and the CD prompts me for my previous installation media, I put floppy number one in the floppy drive and proceed as prompted. Works like a champ. Every time. You will find these ancient floppies at a garage sale, and the guy running the sale will *give* them away. Refrain from indulging in maniacal laughter until you're out of earshot, or otherwise he'll attempt to get you to pay for them.

Now I can just about see a whole crowd of you, sitting out there scratching your heads, wondering, "Why in the name of living hell is this mope going on and on with these ancient and obsolete versions of Windows?"

Good question.

The reason is that the newer versions of Windows are major hogs. The more recent the version of Windows, the more memory and hard drive space the damn thing demands. Free computers will be short on memory and hard drive space. (Remember free computers? They're why this book exists in the first place.)

So short, in fact, that the new Windows won't run on the damn things, which is why somebody gave them away in the first place.

And so, we're going to use the old versions of Windows to help the new owner of her free computer get on the Internet, write that term paper, calculate the entries on that spreadsheet, and all the rest of the swell stuff that computers can do.

Guess what, boys and girls? That old stuff works just fine.

Thank you, Bill Gates.

And, oh yeah, if you should come across a free machine possessed of sufficient horsepower that it will run the latest and greatest, well then by golly I guess that's what you oughtta be loading it with, yes?

Did I really need to just tell you that?

MUST-HAVE SOFTWARE

Internet Browsers

Eighty percent of the reason for having a computer seems to be to let you browse the Internet. This rises to 100 percent for the free computers you'll be giving away. Everybody wants to be able to surf the 'Net, and without a fairly decent Web browser, that's just not gonna happen.

Fortunately, Windows comes with a Web browser already preloaded and ready to go. Load Windows and you've also loaded Internet Explorer—whether you wanted the damn thing or not, in fact. You've actually got to go into the Custom Settings part of your installation routine with Windows and manually disable it if you'd rather not have it—it defaults to installed. Certain Windows don't even have the option to not install it. It's just there, whether you like it or not. Plan on seeing it a lot.

For myself, on my own machine, I don't use it. But then again, my personal machine has the minimal horsepower to run Mozilla, which, admittedly, is a bit of a memory hog. The free computer you're going to be giving away will not have an equivalent amount of horsepower most of the time. At least not for a few more years, that is.

On machines that don't have the moxie to run something a bit improved, old Windows (95 or 98), and the version of Internet Explorer that comes with them, turns out to be a gift from the gods.

Cruddy old 486s with 12 MB of memory and a 200-MB hard drive will sing and dance with an old copy of Windows and the IE that came with it. Maybe not as sleek and shiny as the new stuff, but by god it's WORKING, which is the whole idea, isn't it? Better machines than that will tolerate better software than 95/IE. Push the thing till it chokes and then go with whatever was working one step before you overwhelmed it. Sooner than you think, you'll develop a good feel for what will and will not work in a given rig. When you reach this point, you just load the appropriate software, fire up the machine, and you're done with that part of it.

Once you get good old IE working, you can go out on the Web and Google for different browsers. Download 'em all and see which ones work and which ones you like. The "work" part will be heavily dependent on the precise nature of the machine you're cobbling together from coat hang wire and scotch tape. The "like" part will be heavily dependent on the needs and intelligence of the person you're giving the machine away to. Plan on getting it wrong lots of times and further plan on defaulting to IE, warts and all, most of the time or even all of the time. A major advantage to sticking with the plain vanilla package of Windows and IE is that it increases the odds of getting any useful help when the person that you gave the machine to goes and asks a brother-in-law or somebody like that for advice. More people know about IE than anything else. May as well take advantage of that fact, eh?

Actually getting functionally connected to the Web can be as easy as popping an AOL disk in the slot. Or it can be as difficult as attempting to reach the Web through a firewalled proxy server on a LAN or much, much worse if something decides to conflict with something else somewhere in the bowels of your software, hardware, or both. For the free machines, go ahead and load AOL, pray to the gods of good silicon for forgiveness, and be done with it. What we're doing here is attempting to get people connected. All's fair in love and war.

And while we're on the subject of AOL, it, too, falls under the heading of Free. May as well take advantage. Again. There's other free ways of getting Internet service, but I'm not going to screw up my own deal(s) by blabbing about it here. Some of 'em are short-term, some are long-term, some are more or less legal than others. Some are amazingly faster than others. It should be enough that you're hereby notified that the stuff is out there if you know where and how to look.

Use your street smarts, OK?

And oh yeah, be sure to set your browser's default home page to Google.com.

Antivirals

Going on the Web involves the risk of getting a virus. Or a Trojan, or worm, or whatever arcane term that a particular little beastie might be hung with.

When you see me talking about a virus, think big in terms of the definition for the word "virus." Think of any malware that might come your way, no matter what its official name or description.

Any virus protection software is better than none. And, in a weird sort of way, old antivirals unable to fight the newest threats can sometimes be just as good as the latest edition because you'll be dealing with old hard drives that oftentimes are infected with old viruses. Use old antivirals for checking old hard drives and updated antivirals for loading on machines that will be connecting to the World Wide Whatthehellwasthat and getting exposed to the fresh stuff.

Google around for this software—it's freely available. Download a copy of one of the antivirus programs and save it to a hard drive that you can temporarily hook up to the latest machine you're putting together and then copy it to the main hard drive. Run the installation program on the new machine before you attempt to get online and, once you do get online, immediately invoke the "update" function of the antiviral program to make sure you've got the freshest medicine. That way you stand a sporting chance of avoiding all the trouble that viruses cause.

If a given antiviral program annoys you for any reason, uninstall it and replace it with something that you like better. Don't go running more than one antiviral at a time—the things don't like each other and will likely gum up the works to where your computer won't work any more.

One of the best ways to get a virus is to have an e-mail account of your own, with an Internet service provider of your own. Open the mail, get the virus. I use accounts that free (*that* word again) e-mail providers are so kind as to give away for nothing. I let *their* antivirus programs scan things before mine ever see 'em. I also let their antispam programs filter that out too. If your hotmail account fails to properly filter spam, drop it like a bad habit and go find somebody else's free e-mail service that does a better job blocking uninvited solicitations for breast and penis enlargements at rock-bottom prices.

And unless you specifically requested e-mail with an attachment from somebody, *never* click on attachments to e-mail. Virus, virus, virus!!! If you think there's really something in the attachment that you might need to look at, e-mail the sender of your mystery mail right back and ask if they really sent such and such to you on so and so date. Viruses, worms, and such all are able to spoof you into believing that the very humorous game you just got as an e-mail really did come from your Uncle Bill. Don't believe a bit of it until Bill himself confirms it.

Trojans and worms are sufficiently different that you have to go find a program for them separately. Same deal as with the antivirus programs. More or less.

Firewalls
Something else you'll need for browsing the Web is a firewall. Google that one up too. Like the antivirus programs, there are some nice ones out there to be had for free.

Learn the details of your firewall before you set it loose on a free computer you're giving away. Come to think of it, be sure and do the same with the antivirals. Otherwise, the new owner of the free computer will surely run afoul of this stuff, and her machine will fail to make it to the Internet.

Load this kind of stuff up and then just run it and watch what happens, or doesn't. If it chokes your machine and you can't seem to figure out what's the matter, skip to the next guy's free firewall and start over from scratch (being careful to uninstall the first one before loading the next one).

Putz around here and you'll get it.

Word Processors, Spreadsheets, and the Usual List of Suspects
Office kinds of stuff. Real businesslike. Fine for college folks. Most business wonks already have this crap on the

machine down at the office, paid for by the company.

Try not to load too much of this stuff; nobody needs a whole Office Suite. Not even the wonks down at corporate. This stuff is a major resource hog. Beware.

The word processor is nice and useful though—it lets people send each other letters and stuff. Have a printer handy if you plan on using this kind of program. Tell the guy you give the machine to that the word processor has a spell checker. Then tell him to use it.

Spreadsheets, databases, and all that stuff is almost always a complete waste of time, space, and resources. I suppose if the guy you're giving the machine away to says he wants some of this stuff, and you have the disks lying around to install it with, then go ahead. Otherwise forget it.

Anything that paints pretty colors or allows you to send your Front Page to the Web is total crap and should be dealt with the same way you'd deal with a computer game. Let the recipient of the free computer learn enough about his machine to get hold of this kind of thing on his own and then load it for himself. Tell him it'll build his character to do it that way.

If you wanna play with this stuff on your machine, then go ahead and play with this stuff on your machine. I'm not stopping you.

Copy Software

Although your Windows will copy things just as fine as you please, specialized copy software is still a must. You can't burn a CD without it.

Get hold of a disk or three of good copy programs and hang on to 'em even if you don't have a CD burner. Eventually, you *will* have a CD burner. And when you get it, you'll immediately discover that the thing's worthless without the copy software.

So go ahead and get that stuff now and be done with it.

Spyware

It's not a virus, but it's not your friend either.

Spyware comes in a bewildering array of different sizes, shapes, and intents.

Think of it as something inside your computer watching every place you go on the Web and then reporting that information back to a central computer somewhere far, far away, where greedy hands are being rubbed together in anticipation of receiving that information.

Yeah, this stuff is CREEPY.

Ad-Aware will seek it out and destroy it. So will a few other antispyware programs.

Get one. Or two.

Use 'em.

HOW TOO MUCH SOFTWARE WILL CHOKE A COMPUTER

Computers that work perfectly can still be caused to malfunction merely by having too damned much software loaded.

And I do mean "loaded," as in loaded into memory immediately upon boot-up.

The idiots who write commercial programs seem to believe that unless your machine devotes a fair bit of its memory and hard-drive space to the program *every single time you turn it on*, something is going to come along and cause it to disappear from the face of the Earth.

The software loads up and runs, sort of on idle but certainly using valuable computer resources that would be better spent elsewhere doing something more important. When this stuff is idling away in the background, it enables the main program that it's connected with to load and come to life much faster than it would if it was starting from scratch every time. This makes the main program look good by being a "fast starter" when you press the go button for that program. Sales and marketing folks think this is a good thing, but it comes at a cost; nobody seems to consider anybody else's programs except their own. When there's a bunch of these things all loading and running in the background *every time you start your machine*, the whole system starts to bog down. It will oftentimes take forever to perform the most trivial operations because of the logjam of crap that's hogging all the resources, especially on older machines that are not well endowed with resources in the first place. And again, this is with programs that perform a useful function—stuff like MS Office, printer software, scanner software, what have you. Adware and spyware don't even do anything constructive in the first place. Your machine is bogged down *for no good reason at all.*

Too many things loading at bootup cause a machine to start running sluggishly, and sooner or later this or that program will start to act funny and then not act at all as the encrustations of boot-loaded junk accumulate.

Click start, then run, and then type in msconfig. Click OK.

Click the start-up tab (leave all other tabs *strictly alone*) and see what's listed and further see what's got a checkmark in the little box next to it. Everything with a checkmark in the box loads every single time you start your rig.

Most of that stuff is completely useless loaded that way and will fire right up *just the same* when you click its desktop icon like you're supposed to. Memory is getting gobbled up just to allow AOL to leave a little icon in your systray. Preloaded is *useless* for all but the top two or three programs you use all the time. Give those wasted resources back to your computer so that it can avail itself of them if it needs to for something that actually *counts.*

Boot your machine and check that area right now and see what's hanging out down there. Your firewall oughtta be showing as well as your antivirus. The volume control is good to have, and I've found that the clock is something I can't live without, but everything else is a waste of time.

If you've got a damnable MS Office start-up bar somewhere on your screen every time you start your machine, be sure and eradicate that little monster too!

I run Word every single day, but I still don't need frickin' Office to load its memory-hogging ass into my life on every single boot-up.

Crud from the Internet can only go downhill from where we now sit.

Commercial "enhancements" for your computer (that you stupidly clicked on a popup ad somewhere to check out) are evil and can only make your life worse. Ditto all the rest of that stuff.

Lose it all, soonest!

Why That's Good News for You

Actually, the fact that programs routinely load a bunch of crippling crap into memory is a good thing. At least as long as it's not your computer that's getting the load.

Every single day, friends and strangers are discovering that their machines are acting funny, acting unfunny, or acting dead. When it turns out that the problem consists entirely of an overdose of boot-loaded crapola, the fix is easy. Fire up the machine and have a look at the systray and count the icons. Three or four, tops. If you see a string of icons that goes halfway across the bottom of the screen (yes, I've actually *seen* this) then you've got a pretty good clue that there's a wee bit too much being loaded every time the machine starts up.

Run msconfig and have at it. Whack, chop, hew, lop! There, all better.

If it turns out that something *must* be run at boot-up, then the fix is too easy. Put the check back in the box and go on your merry way.

If you're doing this for someone else, you will look like a wizard. The nice person whose machine you just brought back to full-functioning life will be stoked with what you did and endeavor to thank you. Accept their thanks in more free computers later on, money or sex right now, or whatever seems about right.

Once in a great while people will give a machine away that is suffering from no more than this little malady. Thanks, software guys, for loading all your nonsense into yet another machine.

For Windows XP you also want to go into your services menu and go after all of that stuff too. I highly recommend blackviper.com as a source for all kinds of neat-o ways to improve the performance of your XP machine.

God only knows what's gonna be required when Longhorn (the working name for Microsoft's next OS) comes out. One thing I do know is that there's gonna be yet another wave of "obsolete" computers that get cast aside for me to grab off, gratis.

Thank you, Bill Gates!

Is this a great country or what?

Chapter 5

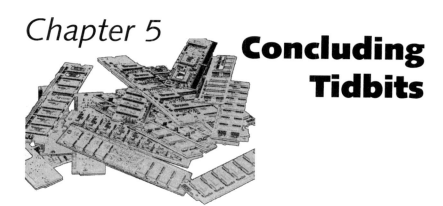

Concluding Tidbits

Well it's all over now except for the shouting, eh?

I hope this helped you.

As for the pointy-headed geek who's shrieking about how stupid and wrong this thing is, I couldn't care less. He already knows all this stuff and has exactly zero business putting his big snout into our book.

I wrote this book in the hopes that at least a few technophobes out there would cast off some of their fear and take a personal plunge into the weird and wonderful world of computers.

The "free" angle is just too good to let get by. It works like a champ and has got to be the most pain*less* and joy*ful* way to embark on this particular mystery tour.

Drink deeply, folks.

I sincerely hope this little starter book was sufficiently nonoverwhelming to allow you to discover that computers are neat-o toys, just like anything else.

After you get into the swing of things, you'll discover that, technically speaking, the pointy-headed geek who's still over there shrieking has a valid point or two (excepting the one on top of his head, of course). By then, however, your entry into the world of computers will have been smooth enough to allow you to find out a thing or two all by yourself, without having to take somebody else's word for it. Which is exactly what I wanted to see in the first place. When your geek muscles start rippling, you too can go to Slashdot and start enlightening the unwashed masses with your plus 2 excellent karma postings, even as you mod trolls down and metamod your fellow Enlightened Ones mods as fair. But go kindly and gently with the noobs, if you please. Those guys are *you* right now, and at no time will you ever be able to appreciate their bewilderment better than right this minute. Take the time, right now, to print upon your brain just what it feels like to have entered this amazingly recondite and ramified parallel universe. Then hold that memory dearly and parcel it out when required over the redounding decades.

Or you could decide to be just another ass and tell 'em all to RTFM.

I wish you today, and those you deal with tomorrow, the best of luck.

Go gently.

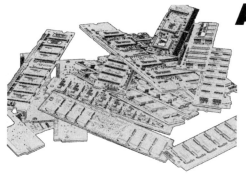

About the Author

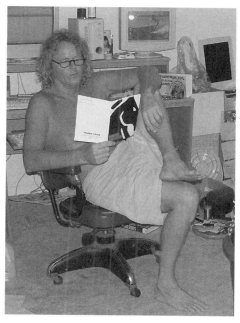

Photo by Crystal Duff

James MacLaren bought his first computer back in 1990 and has never bought a computer since (really!), although he's purchased a peripheral or two over that span of years, but not much. Not much at all.

Working with free machines for his entire computing career has given him a very different perspective on computer operations, maintenance, and repair and has taught him all sorts of real-world arcana at a very accelerated rate. Jim cobbles machines together from giveaway parts just for laughs and then gives them away to people. What fun!